Dimensions of Reading Difficulties

Dimensions of
Reading Difficulties

by A. T. RAVENETTE
Senior Educational Psychologist
London Borough of Newham

PERGAMON PRESS

OXFORD · LONDON · EDINBURGH · NEW YORK
TORONTO · SYDNEY · PARIS · BRAUNSCHWEIG

PERGAMON PRESS LTD.,
Headington Hill Hall, Oxford
4 & 5 Fitzroy Square, London W.1
PERGAMON PRESS (SCOTLAND) LTD.,
2 & 3 Teviot Place, Edinburgh 1
PERGAMON PRESS INC.,
44–01 21st Street, Long Island City, New York 11101
PERGAMON OF CANADA LTD.,
207 Queen's Quay West, Toronto 1
PERGAMON PRESS (AUST.) PTY. LTD.,
19a Boundary Street, Rushcutters Bay, N.S.W. 2011, Australia
PERGAMON PRESS S.A.R.L.,
24 rue des Écoles, Paris 5^e
VIEWEG & SOHN GMBH,
Burgplatz 1, Braunschweig

Printed in Great Britain by A. Wheaton & Co., Exeter

Contents

Acknowledgements

THE author would like to express acknowledgements to the many colleagues in Newham with whom reading has been discussed. He would also like to thank The Monotype Corporation Limited for permission to include Fig. 1, p. 57. He also thanks the National Foundation for Educational Research for permission to print Table 1, p. 15, from *Reading in the Primary School* by J. M. Morris.

The author owes special thanks to Dr. J. H. Kahn, the editor of this series, for his most helpful encouragement and criticisms in writing this book.

Editor's Foreword

THIS book is the first in a new series under the general title "Problems and Progress in Development". It is the intention that each book will take a topic that in the past has been dealt with by a number of different professions, each in its own way, and without knowledge of the contributions that other professions might be making. The aim is to help the different professions to acquire a common language with which to communicate with one another, and to find a framework into which the various contributions could fit together.

The topics that have been selected will come under three headings: Disorders of Function, Critical Stages of Development, and Special Situations.

Disorders of Function refers to difficulties in the acquisition of skills and performance, such as speech, reading, bladder and bowel control, and also the various educational and occupational performances. It can be seen that it will be necessary to take into account constitutional and organic factors, environmental and educational influences, and, amongst the psychological processes, there will be those within the individual as well as the interaction between the individual, his family, and others in the world outside.

Critical Stages of Development will include the landmarks in biological growth and maturation, and cultural adaption. Thus, school entry is a culturally determined event which recognizes progress in childhood development. Puberty marks a biological tage which coincides with the cultural phenomenon of adolescence. The adult stage has its crises of physical, domestic, and occupational life, as have the stages of the climacteric with its anticipation of a somewhat postponed old age in a lengthening span of life.

viii EDITOR'S FOREWORD

Special Situations will refer to family reactions to illness or defect in one member, to changing material circumstances and to events which tend to break up the family unity.

Dr. Ravenette's book deals with difficulties in reading. No topic is more appropriate as an illustration of the infinite variety of explanations and cures for the failure to acquire a skill which is taken for granted as normal. The child who fails to read may be called lazy and be punished, retarded and be coached, mentally defective and be segregated, emotionally disturbed and provided with psychological treatment, dyslexic which merely means having a difficulty in reading, but the word passes for a neurological diagnosis and qualifies the child for special teaching methods. Reading performance itself is a controversial subject, and different teaching methods all have devotees who make claims for the successes of their method with a normal range of pupils and with those who fall below expected levels of performance.

Dr. Ravenette clearly reveals that reading disability is not an entity in itself, and that reading can be studied in different dimensions of human activity and relationships. His approach is original and he searchingly challenges the kind of views which are so frequently given with full professional authority but with no scientific or rational basis. Teachers, paediatricians, psychiatrists, psychologists and social workers are amongst the professional experts likely to be approached, and members of each one of these professions naturally seek an explanation within the general framework of their professional practice. Each explanation and method of treatment is likely to be within a single dimension which ignores all other factors, physical or mental, in the child who lives and grows in his family and social setting. Dr. Ravenette provides a systematic way of considering the various dimensions even when recognizing that one particular dimension has to be chosen for helpful intervention. He provides an example of a logical and scientific method of approach which could be adapted to the study of many other human problems.

No one who reads this book will again be content with snap judgements and easy solutions which depend upon false explanations and which, when they no longer serve, have to be superseded by new false explanations. An explanation is false when it deals with only a fragment of the total experience and ignores the remainder.

Dr. Ravenette takes our attention to the purpose that reading serves in the creation of the child's identity and his feelings of worth. Thus, learning to read, in common with many other acquisitions of skill, represents the intersection of the dimensions in which the child exists and interacts with his family, his teachers, his schoolmates, and the culture generally. He states

> ... primarily reading represents one aspect of the engagement of the child with the life into which he is going, his success in this venture will be crucial in defining the possibilities which are open to him in later life and in defining his own identity amongst his peers, his parents, and his teachers.
> Most children learn to read. Many of these might, in fact, read better than they do. For those who fail we need extra resources of skill, understanding and sympathy. Perhaps we do not have enough of any of these things.

It is a pleasure to offer this book, which can add in so many ways to the "resources of skill, understanding and sympathy" in all those who have responsibility for the nurturing, teaching, and training of children.

J. H. KAHN, M.D., D.P.M.

Introduction

READING requires the existence of technical processes and the knowledge of how to use them. The basic problem is one of representing the spoken word by means of some set of visual symbols. At various times the problem has been solved by the drawing of pictures which stand for situations, at other times conventional signs having some relationship to the objects for which they stand have provided a solution. The spoken language is, however, extremely complex, and the need, therefore, is for a system of visual signs which can carry this complexity. This need is met by the use of an alphabet in which a limited number of conventional signs can be arranged in a wide variety of ways so that they stand for the words, phrases and sentences which we use to carry meaning in our speech.

The existence of some form of alphabet, however, is not in itself sufficient, since it is necessary to have the means for reproducing writing quickly and efficiently and in quantity. The reproduction of the scriptures in the early Middle Ages took years of work even to produce one copy, and the work of copying itself led to the transmission of errors in the text. A truly alphabetic script was probably devised for the first time in about 1300 B.C. (Siu),* but Caxton's printing press was not invented until the fifteenth century.

Reading as a skill for everybody, however, did not become an issue until 1870, when compulsory full-time education was made law. Since that time many reports have been prepared on the state and efficacy of education, and the latest, *Children and their*

* SIU, R. G. H., *The Tao of Science*, Massachusetts, U.S.A.: M.I.T. Press, 1957.

Primary Schools,* encouragingly notes that reading standards have risen considerably in the years since the war. Morris,† however, who carried out an extensive study of children's reading in the county of Kent, argues that one child in every eight leaves school severely handicapped in reading attainment. Standards of literacy are in fact arbitrary. A level which was average in 1949 would now be considered to be well below average. If overall standards improve yearly, standards of backwardness will also be raised yearly. A consideration of the number of children whose attainment is very low does not, however, take into account the number of children whose reading level is far lower than might be reasonably expected from their level of general ability or intelligence. Regardless of absolute figures it is a fact that reading difficulties are very common in our schools even though overall standards may have risen.

It is worth making the point that the inability to succeed in some activity may be of no consequence if nobody is worried about it. The man who likes the atmosphere and companionship of a local pub but who has little skill in the game of darts can frequent those pubs where dart playing is not one of the customs. He is able to choose one where cribbage or dominoes are the pastimes. For him, dart throwing presents no problem as he does not put himself in the position where he is expected to throw darts. Should, however, the ability to throw a "double top" become a necessary qualification for him to enter any pub, this man would find himself in considerable difficulties. At the present time, the ability to read requires, perhaps, a comparable accomplishment.

In the earliest days only handwritten books were available and their readership was restricted to a highly selected few. This was probably still true when printed books became available, but no problems would occur unless the entry to some calling or profes-

---

* Report of the Central Advisory Council for Education (England), London. *Children and their Primary Schools*, H.M.S.O., 1967.

† MORRIS, J. M., *Standards and Progress in Reading*, Slough: N.F.E.R., 1966.

sion depended on skill in reading. Fortunately other occupations could be followed, and a man could elect not to read. Compulsory education, however, completely changed the situation since it involved, amongst other things, the assumption that learning to read and write was within the capacity of all. Moreover, education was a "good" thing and those who failed to learn might be labelled, amongst other things, as "lazy", "immoral" or "ungrateful". These labels are sometimes in use even today, but if we are to use them, we must ask what are the implications for action. It must be recognized that these labels often reflect social attitudes, but it must also be remembered that reading is one of those activities which society expects its citizens to master. Failure to learn is likely to lead to disapproval by parents and teachers. Failures in teaching incur the disfavour of public, press and Parliament. Failure in the eyes of children themselves may lead to feelings of lack of self-esteem, inadequacy of performance or plain despair. And, of course, to be unable to read means diminished employment prospects in adulthood.

Reading difficulties, quite rightly, therefore, are a concern for people whose work involves teaching—teachers themselves, and a variety of professional people who are connected with children. These include doctors, psychologists, psychiatrists, neurologists and many others. The existence of children with reading difficulties is also a concern for administrators and policy-makers both in local authority education departments and in the Department of Education and Science. It is also a problem for parents.

The broad theme of this book is that whoever is asked for help will provide explanations arising out of their training, experience and personal wisdom. In this way, reading difficulties no longer remain a problem exclusively for the child who cannot read, but also for teachers and any other professional workers who may be involved.

Many books and papers have been written on the subject of reading difficulties, each differing in its emphasis. It needs to be stated that the subject-matter which appears in the following chapters also represents a personal choice and personal limitations.

The broad approach is personal but it owes much to the writing of Piaget (see Flavell)* and George Kelly,† each of whom is concerned not only with causes and explanations but also with the problems of how we know and how we understand.

---

* FLAVELL, J. H., *The Developmental Psychology of Jean Piaget*, Princeton: D. Van Nostrand, 1963 (1961).

† KELLY, G. A., *The Psychology of Personal Constructs*, New York: Norton, 1955.

CHAPTER 1

Should we look for Causes and Explanations, or Dimensions in which Observations can be made?

OBJECTS or situations can be understood from widely different points of view. The choice of viewpoint is determined by the experience, interests and training of the viewer. It often happens that an individual finds it difficult to disengage himself from his own point of view either because he holds it too strongly, or because he is ignorant of other viewpoints. The *ego-centric* stage of development described by Piaget* remains as a constant core for adults whether they are professional people or not. There can be no single viewpoint which necessarily provides the best, or even most adequate basis for understanding. What can be seen by one person is only a partial view. What is perceived is only a part of what is perceivable. We can imagine a number of people looking at an old church. An architect will be sensitive to the structure, building materials and the general plan. The clergyman will be sensitive to the building as a place in which the church ritual can be carried out, and the appropriateness of the structure as a place of worship. The historian will be sensitive to the various aspects of the building which reflect changes in styles of building and decoration. Some of these interests he would share with the architect. The photographer will be sensitive to the possibilities of light and shade which will determine such pictures as he might

* PIAGET, J., *Language and Thought of the Child*, London: Routledge & Kegan Paul (English translation 1959), London, 1926.

1

wish to take. Each person would be able to talk with maximum authority about the different aspects to which, by virtue of his training, experience or interest he was sensitive. He could give explanations, build theories or offer practical suggestions about those things which were related to his own speciality. But each one of these people would see a "whole church" only in his own terms. Outside of his speciality, his opinion may be neither better nor worse than that of anyone else.

What is true generally about material phenomena is equally true about the human problems with which we personally have to deal. Any problem can be viewed from a variety of different points of view, and each choice of point of view will reveal something about the viewer as well as something about the problem. What the viewer has to say will spring from his professional orientation, his training and his experience. We deal with our problems out of our own experience and if we cannot find solutions we seek advice from someone, who, we hope, has more appropriate training and experience to cope with these problems. But here there is a difficulty. If an individual has a pain and this pain presents a problem to him, he seeks the help of a doctor. He can only present his problem through the medium of language and the language which is descriptive of pain is very imprecise. As a consequence, the doctor has to elucidate the problem through questions, which are expressed in his own perhaps more precise language. This may not have the same meaning to the person with the pain as to the doctor. The upshot may be that the doctor prescribes some treatment on the basis of a diagnosis which is made on too little information, and the patient leaves the doctor telling himself that the doctor did not understand, or that his questions were stupid. This confusion of meaning may be thought to be trivial, but the implications for action may be of the highest importance.

The significance of this example rests on the fact that information was given and asked for through the medium of language.

The problem which the example poses rests on the fact that the language used by the patient and the language used by the doctor conveyed different meanings. Koestler* suggests that language involves two basic components. The first of these is "matrices",† which refer to the words which make up the language. Within the totality of words which comprise the English language we can recognize that the subject-matter of psychology on the one hand and mathematics on the other use different sets of words. Where the same word appears in each, the meanings are often different. Each subject has a set of words which make up the "matrix". The second component is "codes" and these are the rules whereby words are put together to convey meaning. The rules of grammar represent one code, the rules of meaning represent a different code, e.g *The green cow ate the black grass* makes grammatic sense but does not make semantic sense. The two words green and black need to change places in order to make both grammatical and semantic sense.

In the conversation between the doctor and the patient the language which each used involved rather different matrices, and perhaps rather different codes. In consequence meaningful communication was made more difficult. In ordinary verbal interchanges there is sufficient agreement between the speakers as to the matrices and codes for communication to take place. When, however, there is a problem which involves specialized language there is frequently a considerable gap between the languages of different specialists or between the languages of specialist and layman. This may present a real difficulty where one problem is shared by workers in different professions, since their respective languages may have little in common. There is a further occupational risk in that the professional person may see his own language system as containing the "truth" to the exclusion of the languages of other professional workers. This emotional and intellectual investment in one's own language is frequently

---

* KOESTLER, A., *The Act of Creation*, London: Hutchinson, 1964.

† Koestler uses the expression "matrices", which is technically correct. On the other hand, this same expression is frequently associated with Raven's Matrices, which is a non-verbal intelligence test. The same word has different meanings in different "matrices".

responsible for the failure to appreciate the contributions of others in understanding problems.

In the appraisal of problems by different professions it is necessary, therefore, to evaluate the professional background of those who offer solutions. It must also be recognized that explanations from a single source are at best likely to be only part explanations. In the discussion of reading difficulties an *impasse* has arisen between neurologists and psychologists over the question of whether or not there is such a condition as "specific developmental dyslexia" (word blindness), and so the argument just put forward is not out of place.

The same type of problem may arise between psychologists and teachers if there is not sufficient commonality of experience to bridge the gap between the professional languages used by each.

The discussion so far has been concerned with problems of communication between workers in different professions. It is necessary to turn now to a consideration of some of the difficulties which are inherent to the giving of explanations or causes. In listening to people's conversations the expressions "Oh, he was born that way" or "Well, it's in the family" are frequently heard as explanations. The implication of heredity is that if these explanations are correct there is nothing that can be done about the problem. These same explanations have professional or scientific backing when the statement of causes is prefixed by the words "congenital" or "hereditary". As an example, the condition of "mental defectiveness" can be cited. Because this condition was was either inherited or congenital nothing could be done about "defectives" except to house them in hospitals which were placed a long way from centres of population. A comparable but perhaps more subtle explanation of behaviour is that of "brain damage", and where there is no neurological evidence of brain damage the explanation offered may be "minimal brain damage". The former explanation, quite properly, is made by neurologists, the latter, improperly, by non-neurologists. Explanations of this nature, i.e. using the words "constitutional", or "hereditary" or "congenital" or "organic defect", are not helpful in making decisions about what is to be done. When, however, the search for causes is subordinated to asking what can be done, it is possible to make constructive suggestions which may go some way to resolving problems. Children and adults who are severely sub-normal are now able to receive specialized help which makes the most of their abilities. By asking what can be done much has been learned about how competent they *can* be instead of how disabled they *seem* to be.

Explanations are answers to questions about problems. If the questions refer directly to problems of causation the danger is that the attribution to a cause is taken as putting an end to the questioning. If the question is about what can be done, causation may well be one of several factors and sometimes of only marginal significance. What is important is an evaluation of the problem in all its relevant manifestations.

A word needs to be said about theories since explanations stem from them. Theories are inventions of the mind and they reflect the sense which individuals impose upon their experience of life. Every theory is limited, however, in the range of phenomena for which it can account and, moreover, it is limited in the length of time over which it will be useful. A theory is a fiction which is convenient while it works. In time it will become a mythology as better fictions are invented to replace it. The great danger of theories is that they limit the range of what is meaningfully perceived; yet because of their pragmatic usefulness with regard to certain issues it may be difficult to challenge them. A second danger lies in the fact that sometimes they are responsible for more and more work being done by way of *verification* at the expense of more and more thought about their *practical applications*.

In the light of this discussion it would seem to be advisable to approach the problem of reading difficulties in a different way. The concept "dimension" is familiar in relation to our understanding of space. In that context a dimension is a reference line from which measurements can be made and by means of which objects are defined. Every profession is concerned with sets of issues or problems which can be defined in relation to dimensions which are relevant to that profession, e.g. for doctors the dimension of health or illness is vitally important. The dimensions provide the frame of reference within which problems are understood, and at their simplest represent points of view. The problem of reading and reading difficulties can be seen from a number of different points of view, or dimensions. Each dimension can be used to enlighten the problem and variety of dimensions will enlighten the problem in a variety of ways. No single dimension is necessarily the best, but any one dimension may be more useful in a given instance.

Thinking in terms of dimensions rather than causes has a number of advantages. We must accept the responsibility for the dimensions which we use. The responsibility for causes can frequently be put elsewhere. Dimensions open up areas for exploration, causes frequently become ends in themselves. Dimensions suggest avenues for action, causes in themselves do not. Dimensions are provisional, causes are fixed. In general a dimensional approach offers a freedom both of thought and of action which is absent from an approach which emphasizes causes.

The next chapter will present an overview of the function and purpose of reading but the following chapters will each be concerned with different sets of dimension through which reading difficulties can be understood. Chapter 9 will present an attempt to bring the different dimensions into one overall perspective.

CHAPTER 2

The Function and Nature of the Printed Word

IN THIS chapter we shall take an overview of reading and ask what is the function of the printed word and what are the differences between the language used in speech and the language used in writing.

There is currently a concern as to how efficiently educated and professional people read. A recent book in the Pelican series is entitled *Read Better, Read Faster* and in the introduction there is a sentence, "Why is it the worst readers by any standard are often the ablest of people?" Although this sort of question may make sense to industrial executives and management, a teacher of backward children in a primary school would find it rather surprising. Our concern in this book is not with educated and professional people whose reading skills are inefficient, but with children who from the outset find difficulty even in starting to read, or who later make little progress and may in fact leave school with only the barest level of competency in reading. This presents a problem which is serious for people at all levels of the educational hierarchy, from the Inspectorate to teachers—and for parents.

If we are to understand what is involved in reading we must examine the process at a number of different levels. We must also examine the nature and function of the printed word.

Stated most simply, the printed word provides a means of storing and coding information through the use of visual symbols. These symbols are purely conventional and bear no direct relationship to the information which is to be stored and coded.

Information, or meaning, is deduced from the sequences of symbols. When we learn to read, we learn the conventions embracing both the symbols and the sequences of symbols. When we are competent readers, it may seem to us that the printed text conveys the meaning directly, but in the early stages of learning to read this direct perception is not apparent. Few of us who read well recall learning to read. Yet it was necessary to create a link between visual symbol, auditory symbol and meaning. The auditory link is implicit in almost all printed texts (perhaps least of all in mathematics and symbolic logic), but we do not need to invoke the link once we can read efficiently. At times, in fact, the recognition of the auditory component is a disadvantage in that it slows down the rate of reading, and may inhibit the extent to which we retain what we have read. In the learning stage, however, the auditory link is of fundamental importance.

There is an unfortunate consequence of the arbitrary relationship between the visual and the auditory symbol, i.e. between letter and sound. English is a language where there does not exist a one-to-one correspondence between letter and sound. Very few letters carry the representation of the same sound on all occasions, some combinations of letters stand for a wide variety of different sounds and some sounds may be carried by more than one letter. It is true that there are often rules for determining which sound is correct, but for some combinations the clues can only come from the meaning of the word itself. For example, the sound for *ough* in *bough* could be deduced correctly if the word itself appeared in the context of trees. If, however, we take the complete word *bough* we know that it can also carry the same sound as *bow*—a word which might appear within the context of etiquette and formal courtesies. But *bow* itself carries an alternative sound, and therefore meaning, in the context of *bow* tie, or violin *bow*. If the sound can only be deduced from the meaning which the word is meant to convey a vicious circle is set up whereby without knowing the sound the meaning cannot be known, but the meaning cannot be known because the sound is not known.

This is a real problem in learning to read. Fortunately there are many rules whereby the correct sounds can be deduced, but those who attribute most of children's difficulties in reading to the phonetic problems of language tend to undervalue these rules and also to underestimate the extent to which children are able to learn these rules.

A different set of ambiguities arises from the fact that the visual symbols themselves are not always uniformly presented. Different type faces may be used to present the same letter in different ways, and the relationship to the handwritten letter is not necessarily constant. In learning to read, the letters in their different shapes have to be recognized as invariants with respect to sound but variants with respect to shape, e.g. g, g, G or A, a, ɑ. We also use the convention of "capital" letters, which signify the start of a sentence, and also for proper names. Moreover, the capital letters are usually used when teaching the names of the letters to children although the sound represented by the letter is different. The sound of a word is seldom created correctly by saying the names of the letters. Some children, it is true, are able to deduce the word correctly from the names of the letters, but at best it is an inefficient technique, and one where the possibility of error is at a maximum. For a child to be able to say the alphabet is no guarantee of ability, or readiness, to read. It may even be a serious handicap. But many parents teach their children this, and many children's books seem to perpetuate the problem.

Thus, when we consider the printed word as a visual code for storing information, we can see that there is a host of ambiguities which have to be mastered both in the recognition of the visual appearance, and in the auditory sound picture.

But the information storage aspect of the printed word is only a part of the problem. The printed word provides a means of communicating between one person and many other persons regardless of time and space. A book written thousands of years ago, and in a different language, can be available to any single individual now—and in the future. The temporal gap between the writer and ourselves is bridged by the printed word, and the language gap is reduced by translation. The book is a means of communication, but with a difference. When communication takes place in a face-to-face situation the process is two-way. The speaker obtains feed back from the listener. In this way the speaker can modify what he is saying by observing the reactions of the listener. The printed word does not provide for this. In listening to someone's speech we have help in understanding what he is saying by observing his gestures, his intonation and his pauses. These aids are denied when we read. There is a responsibility therefore placed on the writer to present his ideas in such a way as to be readily understandable. The difficulty is present even in writing this account of the problem. The choice and sequences of words must carry the message. The writer gets no feed back from the reader and in the same way the reader gets no auxiliary feed back from the writer. The consequence is that printed words constitute a different language system from that of the spoken word. Many words used in writing may, in fact, hardly ever be used in conversation, and the sequence of words of a printed message, if spoken aloud in conversation, might well fail to hold the listeners' attention and would in any case probably be thought to be artificial and pedantic.

Vigotsky (1934, 1962),* whose writings on thought and language are very relevant in this context, says: "Written speech is a separate linguistic function, differing from oral speech in both structure and mode of functioning." Relating this idea to children's learning, he says "our studies show that he (the child) has little motive to learn writing when we begin to teach it. He feels no need for it and has only a vague idea of its usefulness. *In every conversation, every sentence is prompted by a motive. Desire or need lead to request, question to answer, bewilderment to explanation.*" Acceptance of the truth of this in relation to the child's creation of the written word leads to recognizing related problems in his understanding of the written word. What the young child reads bears little relation to his natural use of

* VIGOTSKY, L. S., *Thought and Language,* Massachusetts: M.I.T. (1st English translation), 1962.

language. What he would himself express in a few words is presented at great length in printed words. And he may find that the use of so many extra words in the redundancy of print may seem almost as foreign as a foreign language.

Up to this point the printed word has been discussed as a code, and as a means of communication. It is also necessary to look at the information which is coded and stored, or at what it is that is being communicated. In other words, why should the information be stored and communicated? Put more simply, why should people read?

Perhaps the best answer can be given by reference to the largest source of the printed word which we now know, that is the daily newspaper. The daily paper fulfils a number of functions. It provides factual information about what is happening in the world, either locally or nationally. It provides entertainment through its stories, its gossip and its puzzle features. It provides factual matter related to living—cooking, dressing, buying and so forth. It provides hope for betterment through its horoscopes, betting tips and pools forecasts. It provides for the owners of the newspapers ways of attempting to modify people's attitudes and beliefs through the way it reports facts and through its comments on the facts. In other words, the printed word offers to anybody and everybody ways of broadening, or confirming, their interests, hopes and predilictions. Any of these different aspects can, of course, be followed up in with less ephemeral material by reading books.

Although newspapers provide a source of information which is produced every day of the week and which is available to everyone, it does not follow that everyone takes advantage of everything that is offered. People select what is relevant for their own purposes. Different newspapers offer different fare and produce it in accordance with what the proprietors think the readers want. Reading provides a means of furthering an individual's interest or needs. Without such needs or interests there would be no reason for an individual to read or to learn to read.

It is doubtful if any of these functions of the printed word are particularly relevant to children learning to read, although infant teachers use the idea of the daily newspaper, as created by the children themselves, as an important teaching device. Yet, without skill in reading, the child is seriously handicapped in the extent to which he can study other subjects. In practice he must learn to read in order to acquire proficiency in all aspects of education at school. The child who fails in reading therefore needs special facilities if he is to receive the maximum benefit from school.

If this is a primary justification for reading, reading at a later stage is absolutely necessary as the means whereby our daily lives are regulated by the codes of society or of the government. Speech itself provides the child with a means of regulating his behaviour, and reading is an extension of this function. School rules, notices, announcements appear in print. Rules related to our conduct of living appear in formal announcements from the Inland Revenue, from insurance companies, hire purchase agents, from local authorities. Not to be able to comprehend the printed word puts the individual at a disadvantage among his peers, at a disadvantage in a court of law, where ignorance is no plea, and sometimes in material affairs. When rate relief recently became available for certain low-income house tenants, very few applied. When some who should have been eligible for benefits were questioned as to why they had not applied they said they had not read the various printed notices in the local papers, and on notice boards, which advised them of this relief. These people could read, but felt no need to read. Perhaps it should not be taken for granted that to have learned to read is enough. People only read what they easily perceive is relevant—and then it must be in a form which is comprehensible.

At a more sophisticated level, reading provides a means for the adult to escape for a while from everyday life by way of novels, plays, poetry and a variety of other literary forms. The book in fact becomes a major factor in the way leisure is spent. The use of books for adult study is as sophisticated as their use for aesthetic enjoyment.

These justifications are hardly necessary for the adult reader, but it is very doubtful if they have much relevance for the infant school child who has the task of learning to read. The child, in fact, has to learn a skill the use of which will only become apparent later, but the learning has to come first. Hence the need for reading to be made relevant and perhaps a failure in this may lead to a failure in learning.

Finally, reading is a social skill. To be literate in present-day society is to be normal, even if one does not in fact read. To be illiterate is to be abnormal and to be abnormal is to be at a serious disadvantage. But not only is reading a social skill, it is also a means of becoming socialized. Not to be socialized is to run the risk of being isolated, unemployed and anti-society. To be able to read reduces this risk.

CHAPTER 3

The Causes of Reading Failure as described by Head Teachers

HAVING looked at the nature and the function of the printed word we can now turn to a consideration of the ways in which head teachers understand the causes of reading failure. Teachers and head teachers are, apart from the parents, the people who have the most intimate relationship with children, and who are in the best position to observe the learning process as it takes place when children learn to read. They are also well placed to assess the parents and the family backgrounds of individual children. It should not be assumed, however, that they have the same sorts of specialized knowledge and approach as perhaps a social worker. Consequently teachers' observations of the family background will depend on their sensitivity and on the willingness of parents to confide in them. The other aspect of the situation which teachers know best is the school itself, its staffing, the quality of the staff and the provision of the educational materials. It is not surprising, therefore, that the major dimensions which teachers use to describe reading failure relate to factors within the child, factors within the home, and factors within the school. What is of more particular interest is the extent of which factors in each dimension are felt to contribute to the problem of reading failure.

Two sources of evidence are available. The author conducted an inquiry amongst head teachers in the London Borough of Newham in which they were asked to give three causes of reading failure and three causes of reading success. Morris,* as part of a larger inquiry into reading in Kent, asked head teachers to give

* MORRIS, J. M., *Reading in the Primary School*, London: Newnes, 1959.

14

seven reasons for children's failure in reading. The second inquiry is presented first since it is in some ways more exhaustive and it also antedates the Newham inquiry.

Sixty head teachers were involved in the Kent study. Although Morris elicited fifty different reasons, most head teachers limited their response to three or four. It would be interesting to know why some head teachers were content with three or four reasons when seven were asked for and only some gave seven reasons. Perhaps most head teachers felt that three or four were adequate, perhaps the experience of some was limited, or perhaps the samples of children in the different schools were such as to reduce the number of reasons necessary to explain reading failure. To answer these questions would require a different sort of inquiry.

Morris coded the reasons which were given into three broad categories: causes within the child, causes within the home, and causes within the school. As the head teachers were asked to give their reasons in order of importance it is possible to tabulate the frequency with which each category was given and also its degree of importance. These are given in Table 1.

TABLE 1

FREQUENCY AND IMPORTANCE OF THE CAUSES OF READING DIFFICULTIES
ACCORDING TO 60 HEAD TEACHERS

Causes	Frequency and degree of importance							Total
	a	b	c	d	e	f	g	
1. Centred in child	47	22	21	12	9	2	1	114
2. Centred in home	5	25	20	9	1	1	1	62
3. Centred in school	8	12	13	5	3	1	0	42

In this table the letters (a) to (g) stand for the degree of importance attributed to any category, and the numbers in the columns represent the frequency with which each category was given, e.g. forty-seven head teachers gave some cause operating within the child as the main reason and twenty-five gave causes centred on the home as the second reason.

This analysis is very interesting, showing as it does that over half of the reasons given refer to causes thought to be located in the child. The roles of home and school are seen to be of secondary importance both in the absolute numbers, and in the fact they appear in columns (b) and (c) rather than in column (a).

Morris breaks down each of these categories into specific factors in a table which is not reproduced here. Causes within the child are predominantly related to low intelligence. A cause of this kind appeared as the most important single reason for forty-three head teachers. Physical disabilities (hearing and speech, vision, etc.) account for twenty-five reasons, but never as of first importance. "Personality" accounts for twenty-four reasons, but there is no special emphasis on any particular aspect of personality. Lack of interest, or of desire to read, appears as the major reason only once. Problems of attendance or change of school provide thirteen reasons with the degree of importance ranging from (a) to (e).

Causes centred on the home are primarily concerned with "lack of encouragement", which is given thirty-two times. "Poor cultural background" is given nine times, but in fact, many of the remaining reasons reflect other aspects of a poor cultural background.

Causes located within the school are divided equally between the use of inappropriate teaching methods and problems concerned with teachers themselves. Problems of organization account for ten of the reasons given.

A possible generalization from these data is that the Kent teachers used two major dimensions in understanding reading failure. The first and foremost dimension for them was in terms of lack of intelligence and the next was in terms of lack of encouragement at home. Other factors were recognized but they were not given the degree of importance of the first two. This analysis may, of course, be relevant for the particular set of teachers in a particular area. Comparable questions in a radically different area might produce different results.

The county of Kent would include families of widely different social background, ranging from upper middle class to lower working class. The Borough of Newham, on the other hand, is a predominantly working-class area. This difference between the two areas might lead to head teachers perceiving reading difficulties differently. It was also felt to be a useful idea to find out if head teachers saw reading success and reading failure as determined by the same factors. Hence the Newham head teachers were also asked to give three reasons which they thought determined reading success. Twenty-two head teachers replied and it was interesting that two of these responded only to failure questions and two only to the success questions.

The responses were classified into the same categories as those used by Morris, i.e. causes focused on the child, causes focused on the home and causes located within the school. Head teachers were not asked to put their reasons into an order of importance so it is not possible to present the results with the same detail as is given in Table 1. The frequencies, however, for each set of causes are given in Table 2 and the corresponding totals for the Kent teachers are given for comparison purposes.

TABLE 2

FREQUENCIES OF CAUSES FOR READING DIFFICULTIES AND READING SUCCESS GIVEN BY TWENTY-TWO NEWHAM HEAD TEACHERS TOGETHER WITH COMPARISON TOTALS GIVEN BY SIXTY KENT HEAD TEACHERS

Causes	For failure	For success	Kent teachers' failure
Within the child	35 (57·4%)	34 (55·5%)	114 (52·3%)
Within the home	13 (21·3%)	20 (32·8%)	62 (28·5%)
Within the school	13 (21·3%)	7 (11·5%)	42 (19·3%)
Total	61	61	218

When the frequencies of the reasons given for failure in reading in each of the inquiries are compared the agreement on causes focused within the child is striking. The proportion is almost the same. Moreover, those differences which appear in relation to home and school causes are too small to be considered as other than chance variations. An examination of the replies also suggested that these causes within the child were thought to be lack of intelligence rather than any other. On the other hand, causes within the home were tied to factors in the cultural background more than to lack of encouragement.

A comparison of the frequencies of the different sorts of reasons given for success as opposed to failure shows that, for practical purposes, the proportions are the same. Such differences as do exist are more likely to be chance variations rather than significant differences. Success and failure, therefore, are seen by head teachers to be related to the same factors. General ability, the main factor centred in the child, is seen to be the major determinant; factors at home will be important modifiers of success or failure, and factors within the school are seen to have the least effect. Whilst this statement reflects the overall meaning of the data it is unsatisfactory as an explanation. Head teachers were asked to give discrete reasons for success and failure. They were not asked how different causes interacted with one another to produce success or failure. Burt (1937)* argued forcefully that there must always be at least two factors involved in reading failure since there is no single cause which is absolutely related to reading ability. Some children with high general ability read poorly, some with low general ability read well. Some children with good home backgrounds read poorly, some with bad home backgrounds read well. In the best schools there are some poor readers, in the worst schools there are some good readers. It would perhaps have been more profitable to ask head teachers what combinations of causes they thought would lead to success or failure. We can assume, however, that when head teachers presented their reasons they might well have in mind a variety of factors which were interrelated. Some of the Newham head teachers, in fact, showed that they thought in just that way, and this could be seen in the way in which they detailed their reasons.

* BURT, C., *The Backward Child*, London: University of London Press, (1937, 1967).

Looking at reading failure first, five of the teachers gave reasons related solely to factors within the child or solely to factors external to the child. For these teachers, therefore, some of these factors were apparently irrelevant, in theory, if not in practice. On the other hand, another five teachers gave reasons related to each of the three factors described as major, viz. ability, home factors and school factors. One would suspect that teachers in these two groups would use different strategies in dealing with the reading problems with which they were faced.

Looking next at reasons for success in reading a different pattern emerges. Sixteen gave general ability as the first determinant. Of these, six gave personality as the second determinant and five gave home factors as the third determinant. The surprising part of this finding is the omission of the school as a determinant of reading success. Why should head teachers see the school situation as partly responsible for failure and yet, at the same time, not take some of the credit for success? Another difference emerges in relation to success in that only two head teachers gave reasons that were solely internal, or solely external to the child.

The data provided by these two inquiries should not be taken as hard facts about the "causes" of reading failure. They provide information concerning the head teachers' explanations of reading success and failure. The overwhelming importance attributed to factors within the child probably reflects the fact that the teachers' job is with children—understanding children and teaching them. As a consequence, they will be maximally sensitive to problems arising with children and within children. It is important to know the implications of these ways of construing, or understanding, reading failure.

It will be recalled that the most important single reasons that head teachers gave was lack of general ability or intelligence. If the view is taken that intelligence is an innate attribute, largely determined by heredity, and not amenable to environmental modification, then to give lack of intelligence as a cause of reading failure is tantamount to saying that there is little that can be done about it. It is, of course, doubtful if head teachers are committed to this belief completely, but if the view is held at all, there is a risk of holding a defeatist attitude towards children of low ability. This, in turn, would lead to teaching practices that would result in confirming the view.

If, on the other hand, the view is taken that environmental resources can be used to make good a child's disability (Vigotsky, (*op. cit.*, Hunt* and Bernstein†), then it becomes possible for a head teacher to devise strategies within a school that are designed not only to develop the ability to read, but also that general ability which is called intelligence.

Turning to factors within the home, a comparable choice is offered. If the view should be taken that home conditions are basically unmodifiable, or that a head teacher has no authority to try to modify the home factors, then giving factors within the home as causes of reading failure, is to say also that there is nothing that can be done about it. On the other hand, a head teacher who takes an active role with parents is likely to attempt ways whereby parents can and do change their attitudes to the school and to the education process. In this case, teachers would expect concurrent changes both in reading ability and in the home background.

It might seem that factors within the school are very much under the control of the head teacher. This is not, in fact, true. In times of serious staff shortages, a head teacher may have to make do with whatever staff is available. This staff may be ill-equipped to deal with the reading problems that are present even with children of average ability. There may be shortages of material resources which may stem from local authority financial policy, or, at times of national economic crises, of governmental policy. Under these conditions, the head teacher may have to make the best of a poor situation in terms of staff, of materials, and sometimes even of buildings. Nevertheless he may be able to achieve the development

* HUNT, J. McV., *Intelligence and Experience*, New York: Ronald Press, 1961.

† BERNSTEIN, B., Language and social class. *Brit. J. Sociol.*, **11**, 271–6, 1960. *A Socio-linguistic Approach to Social Learning*. In Penguin Survey of the Social Sciences, Penguin Books, Harmondsworth, 1965.

of an atmosphere in which reading success is expected, and where reading failures are not rejected. This in itself is a big achievement and is as important as the material aspects of the school situation.

In this chapter we have looked at the three major dimensions which head teachers use in their descriptions of the development of reading failure. The subsequent chapters will take up these dimensions in greater detail and will also show how different aspects of each of these dimensions can be related to the concepts used by different professional workers who are also involved in understanding reading difficulties.

CHAPTER 4

Dimensions
within the Child—Cognitive Factors

THE broad dimensions which were outlined in the previous chapter provide an appropriate framework for the following chapters. Although there is little evidence which specifically relates difficulties within the child, within the home and within the school other than on a statistical basis—the interrelationships need always to be borne in mind. Burt* argues that in cases of reading difficulty at least two factors must be looked for, since there is no single disability which bears a perfect relationship with reading attainment. For every child with a specific handicap who cannot read, there are plenty more with the same handicap who can. Whilst ideally we need to look for combinations of dimensions we shall in fact examine the various dimensions as if they were separate. In this chapter we shall look at cognitive factors within the child, i.e. those factors which head teachers presented most frequently as the basic causes of reading difficulty. These factors are those in which psychologists tend to be interested, and consequently we shall be very much concerned with the psychologists' dimensions of reading and reading difficulty.

Before proceeding with this, however, it is necessary to look at the process of reading itself in order to see what particular skills a child needs to have available in order to be able to learn. This will provide a background against which the various cognitive abilities can be assessed.

Reading involves recognition of rather complex and detailed

* BURT, *op cit*. (1937).

visual symbols and relating these to complex auditory sounds. It is clearly necessary, therefore, that a child's sensory equipment should be sufficiently developed to cope with this task, and to a great extent this depends on physiological maturation. This is not entirely true since appropriate experience may well facilitate development of the neuro-muscular apparatus, e.g. eye/hand co-ordination. The print which is used in books for young children is usually much larger than that which is used for older children and adults. None the less, the print calls for a rather fine discriminative ability. Doman* has made much of this by suggesting that children from the age of 2 years and upwards can learn to read if they are presented with really large print, and some of his evidence suggests that from the point of view of word recognition this may be true. Discrimination of sounds involves an equally fine ability, and this does not depend on auditory acuity alone. For the child the unit of sound tends to be complete phrases rather than separate words or the sounds which make up a word. It is doubtful if even adults hear each word as a separate unit. In learning to read, however, the child has also to learn to deal with small and discrete auditory units, e.g. single words, and then single letters, and their sounds. In order to achieve this he has to be able to analyse both visual and auditory stimuli, and then to synthesize them. These are separate abilities not necessarily related, and may well be a function of what is normally called general ability or intelligence. At the same time, words within sentences and letters within words follow a sequence which in print in European languages proceeds from left to right. The child has to cope with this sequence and has to be able to retain information in his memory from the beginning of the sequence in order to make sense of the whole sequence. When children build up words by their constituent letters, it is not uncommon for them to forget the beginning sounds by the time they reach the end sounds. When this happens they cannot possibly work out what the word is and usually guess or give up. Not only is this memory capacity very important within the actual learning

* DOMAN, G. J., *Teach your Baby to Read*, London: Cape, 1965.

situation, but also the child also has to be able to store information from day to day, from week to week, and from month to month.

Many of these abilities contribute to the development of that general ability which is commonly called intelligence, but the child can fail in any, and the failure needs to be recognized by the teacher. They may be crucial in the early stages of learning to read.

When new words are learned it is frequently the case that they appear some five or six times in slightly different contexts within a few pages of text. It is assumed, and it may in fact be true, that this is a sufficient number of repetitions for a child to learn the words. The evidence of teachers of children in schools for educationally subnormal pupils suggests that eight or nine repetitions may be necessary for such children for a word to be mastered. It would seem then that children will vary in their need for repetition in the texts that the school provides. This again is probably related to the child's intellectual status.

At a later stage new words are frequently recognized and learned according to the contexts in which words appear, i.e. the sense provided by the known words will determine the likelihood of what the unknown word should be. Clues within the word itself can be used to confirm the child's deduction. This is a very satisfactory method of learning, but the child who has no skill in understanding the context, or no skill in sounds to confirm his hunch, is not likely to make much progress without help. All the initial skills previously mentioned are important at this stage, and without them the child is handicapped.

Meanwhile the child who is learning, as opposed to failing, is speeding up his reading just because he knows more words and is able to comprehend the context. Slowness creeps in, however, if the child continues to use the analytic skills which were necessary at an early stage but which should be discarded as he progresses, and this may well happen where there is a parallel failure of comprehension. This becomes a vicious circle since slowness itself will make comprehension more difficult.

When reading is well established as a skill the reader does not read every word as a discrete entity, but takes in phrases and sentences at a glance. He may well skip parts of the text but still retain the essential meaning. At this point some specialized training may be necessary in order to increase reading efficiency, but this problem falls outside our immediate concern. Broadly speaking, children's difficulties arise mainly in the *early* stages of learning to read, but they may reappear at later ages when the reading material becomes more complex. There may also be problems when a reading level of about 7 years is reached, at which stage new skills of comprehension become important. There are also reading difficulties which occur in the secondary school with children who have not been recognized in the primary school as being in need of special help.

Reading Ability and Intelligence

It has long been recognized that there exists a relationship between intelligence and the ability to read. Gates* argued that "The standard Binet type tests with certain reading exercises eliminated, provides the best general criterion of verbal or linguistic aptitude or ability in oral comprehension with which achievement in reading may be compared". Whilst this statement is broadly true, there are a number of theoretical and practical problems which arise when we attempt to measure and correlate intelligence and reading ability.

It is worth making the point that *intelligence* is a concept, not a thing in itself. *Intelligence* is an abstraction from behaviour which meets certain criteria for accuracy, or speed or appropriateness. The criteria are often determined by reference to established conventions, e.g. a dictionary definition of words, or by consensual agreement, e.g. a response which most people would make. Whilst there is a certain pragmatic usefulness in such a concept as intelligence, it raises as many problems as it solves. Currently in fact it has come under considerable attack by those workers

* GATES, *The Improvement of Reading*, New York: Macmillan, 1935.

who are concerned with *creativity* (Getzels and Jackson,* Hudson,† Wallach and Kogan‡.

At a purely theoretical level it is possible to talk about intelligence in abstract terms. At the practical level, however, we are faced with a number of difficulties. It is seldom the case that an individual will obtain identical scores on two different tests of intelligence. This arises from the fact that different tests are measuring different things. It is true that individuals who do well on one test will tend to do well on a different test, but it is common to find wide differences as well. Given widely different scores on different tests, what is it possible to say about an individual's intelligence as an integral quality? We have in fact to recognize that an individual can work intelligently in some ways, comparatively unintelligently in other ways. This, of course, is common sense. But a discrepancy between a person's score on different tests may provide a gateway to better understanding of that person, and this approach is very relevant when we try to relate reading attainment to levels of intelligence.

There are also problems of measurement. The extent to which ability as measured by one test is related to ability according to measures on a different test is estimated by the correlation coefficient. This is an index ranging from $1 \cdot 0$, which indicates complete agreement between scores, through $0 \cdot 0$, which indicates a random level of agreement, to $-1 \cdot 0$, which indicates complete negative agreement. This occurs when the top score on one test is associated with the bottom score on the other test. The significance of the correlation coefficient, i.e. the extent to which it represents a relationship closer than would be expected purely by chance, however, depends on the size of the sample from which it is calculated. A very small correlation from a very large sample can be highly significant, a very large correlation from a very small sample might be no better than chance.

* GETZELS, W. and JACKSON, P. W., *Creativity and Intelligence*, New York: Wiley, 1962.

† HUDSON, L., *Contrary Imaginations*, London: Methuen, 1966.

‡ WALLACH, M. L. and KOGAN, N., *Modes of Thinking in Young Children*, New York: Holt, Rinehart & Winston, 1965.

The practical value of the correlation coefficient stems from the fact that it enables a prediction to be made from a score on one test to a score on the other, while at the same time it provides a measure of the range of most likely scores to be expected on the second test. The larger the correlation, the more confidence there is in the prediction which can be made. If, however, the sample from which the correlation is calculated is limited in some way, e.g. a narrow age range, or a narrow ability range, then the correlation is likely to be lower than for a less homogeneous or restricted sample.

These problems can be illustrated by two studies (Ravenette* and one unpublished), where the practical purpose was to select children who were to be given special help in remedial reading centres. The theoretical argument stemmed from the belief that a measure of verbal ability was the best way of predicting reading success. The necessary data were collected by testing children from the second, third and fourth years in primary schools. One test was the Crichton Vocabulary Scale (Raven†) in which children had to define words), the other test was the Schonell Graded Word Reading Test (Schonell)‡—in which children had to read a series of disconnected words. There were about thirty children in each age group, and the correlation for each was of the order of about 0·5. This would lead to predictions of reading age only within rather broad limits. To make the predictions with greater specificity, the age groups were combined and the effect of this was to increase the correlation, and hence the predictive value, to 0·75. With this correlation, it could be calculated that for any given level of verbal ability, as defined by the ability to define words correctly, 68% of the children would have reading ages which fell between the actual predicted reading age for that level

* RAVENETTE, A. T., Vocabulary level and reading attainment: an empirical approach to the assessment of reading retardation. *Brit. J. Educ. Psychol.* **31,** 96–103 (1961).

† RAVEN, J. C., *Guide to Using the Crichton Vocabulary Scale,* London: Lewis, 1950.

‡ SCHONELL, F. J., *Diagnostic and Attainment Tests,* Edinburgh: Oliver & Boyd, 1950.

plus or minus 1·2 years of reading age. For example, if the predicted reading age for vocabulary score of 40 was 9 years, then 68% of children with that vocabulary score would have reading ages falling between 7·8 years and 10·2 years. This, it can be seen, is a wide margin of tolerance. Had we worked from the data for each year group separately, then the margin of tolerance would have been greater still.

In the second study two tests of vocabulary were used, that which has already been described, and the English Picture Vocabulary Scale (Brimer and Dunn),* in which children have to point to one of four pictures which represents a word that the child is told. One major difference between the two tests is that for the former demands are made on a child's verbalizing ability, whereas for the latter the child does not have to speak at all. The age range of this sample was 7-year– and 8-year-old children and there were 124 in the sample. The correlation between each vocabulary test and reading attainment this time was 0·57, based on pooling the data for both year groups. Using this correlation it was found that for any given level of ability (on either test) 68% of the children had reading ages between the predicted reading for that level plus or minus 1·7 years. This is a much wider range of tolerance than for the first study, and had we worked from each year group separately the margin would have been wider still.

If we accept as normal for a given level of ability the predicted reading age plus or minus 1·7 years, then we can ask if children whose reading ages exceed these limits for one of the vocabulary tests also exceed these limits for the other vocabulary test. In fact, of thirty-two children whose reading ages fell below these limits for either test, only fourteen had reading ages which fell below those limits on both tests. Comparable figures were found for children whose reading ages were above the limits. If we argue that children whose reading ages are too low for their level of ability need special remedial help, it follows that the selection of such children depends on the test that is used as the criterion.

* BRIMER, M. A. and DUNN, M. L., *English Picture Vocabulary Test*, Slough: N.F.E.R., 1966.

When, therefore, we say that intellectual ability is a major dimension in determining reading attainment, some important qualifications need to be made. In the first place, the measured relationship between intelligence and reading attainment depends very much on the nature of the sample. With a wide age range the relationship is likely to be much more marked than with a small age range. Moreover, if the ability range is limited, the relationship may well be extremely small. It is common experience that the relationship between measured intelligence and final reading age amongst pupils in schools for the educationally sub-normal is extremely low. In other words, a high level of intelligence at entry is no guarantee of success in reading at the age of 16 years. The implication of these qualifications is that age and level of intelligence operate together in determining the measured relationship between intelligence and reading. How this inter-action changes is not clear. Schonell* suggests that the relationship between the two variables decreases with age and quotes correlations of $0 \cdot 79$ at 8 years, $0 \cdot 58$ at 9 years, $0 \cdot 59$ at 10 years and $0 \cdot 44$ at 11 years. He does not indicate the intelligence tests that were used. On the other hand, Fransella and Gerver,† with a sample of children referred to the Maudsley Hospital, by no means necessarily on account of educational or reading problems, found that the correlation between intelligence (as measured by the W.I.S.C. Verbal Intelligence Scale) and reading attainment increased with age, but the correlation between chronological age and reading attainment decreased with age. The data presented earlier in the chapter relating vocabulary and reading also show an increase in the relationship with age. The picture is likely to be complex.

A second set of qualifications of the attribution of reading attainment to intellectual ability stem from the fact that different measures of intelligence will lead to the recognition of different

* SCHONELL, F. J., *Backwardness in the Basic Subjects*, Edinburgh: Oliver & Boyd, 1942.

† FRANSELLA, F. and GERVER, D., Multiple regression equations for predicting reading age from chronological and W.I.S.C. Verbal IQ. *Brit. J. Educ. Psychol.* **35**, 86–9 (1965).

groups of retarded readers. This need not be a disadvantage if more than one measure of intelligence is used since difference in scores between the different intelligence tests may give some indication of cognitive differences which may be related to reading failure. The basic assumption underlying this approach is that perhaps we need to stop assuming that all we have measured is intelligence and start looking for all of the attributes that a test may be measuring. As Payne* argues, the more an individual might appear to be deviant from the group that is being tested, the more likely is a test score to be determined by factors other than "intelligence".

A final set of qualifications arises from a consideration of the form of administration of tests. The real problem arises when group tests are used, since with these it is not possible to retain control of all the factors which might affect a test score. These factors involve the child's understanding of what to do both in terms of the test content and in terms of practical requirements, e.g. put marks in the correct places, not missing out items, etc. Under these circumstances the final score of an individual child may be an amalgam of a variety of factors, none of which is built into the structure of the test. Whilst it is possible to discuss how a group of children has performed, there is much less assurance about the performance of the individual child, the more so if he is already deviant from the group by reason of reading difficulties. The younger the children who are tested, the less reliable any measured relationship will be since young children are puzzled by the formality of formal testing in the classroom and, moreover, the lowest levels of tests are often too high for the dullest children. This is especially true of reading tests, which may have as the starting-point for measurement an assumed reading age of 4 years (Burt), 5 years (Schonell Graded Word Reading Test), 5 years 9 months (Holborn Reading Scale) or 6 years (Neale).

An example which can be criticized on all the points which have

* PAYNE, R. W., Cognitive abnormalities, in *Handbook of Abnormal Psychology* (ed. H. J. EYSENCK), London: Pitman Medical Pub. Co., 1960.

been made is a research note by Savage and O'Connor.* The children were aged 6·9 to 7·9 years. The intelligence test was a group non-verbal test. The reading test was a sentence reading test. The outcome of the investigation was an observed correlation between intelligence, as measured by this particular test, and reading attainment of 0·380. Whilst this relationship is undoubtedly real it is not very large for predictive purposes, but even if it were, there would be good grounds for questioning the results. The floor, or lowest measurable level, of the reading test might be satisfactory for second- or third-year primary children, but is high for first-year children. These children are not uniformly sophisticated in being tested, and it is not known what effect this might have had. Although we have a statistically reliable relationship, it is difficult to know just what it means in behavioural terms.

In general, therefore, whilst it is true that children who are intelligent can usually read, the spread of reading attainment for any one level is so broad as to indicate that very many other factors must also be involved. Age, of course, is just such a factor. Further, the precise measurement of the relationship between reading and intelligence is itself problematic since it is sensitive to the age and homogeneity of the sample, to the nature of the test itself and to the form of administration. Thus, if we are faced with the problem of selecting children for special help, we need a great deal of empirical information about the reading attainment/intelligence level relationship in order to select effectively. Finally, if we are concerned with explanation, the concept of intelligence *per se* adds nothing to our understanding unless we can specify more precisely how this intelligence manifests itself as part of the learning process in reading.

Other Cognitive Factors

Although head teachers considered that lack of intelligence was the major determinant of reading disability they also listed

* SAVAGE, R. D. and O'CONNOR, D. J., The assessment of reading and arithmetic attainment in school. *Brit. J. Educ. Psychol.* **36**, 317–18 (1966).

physical disabilities such as defects of vision, hearing and speech. These are usually recognized and are dealt with by the School Health Department. Occasionally they do go unrecognized, in which case they may create generalized learning difficulties. A distinction needs to be made, however, between *defects* such as these and *difficulties* in visual and auditory perception. Eyesight and hearing may be perfectly normal, yet an individual may be restricted in his meaningful perception, visual or auditory, of incoming stimuli.

Vernon,* who provides the most detailed review of research on reading difficulties, offers three pages only on intelligence, but gives a chapter each on visual and auditory perception. This is an interesting reversal of values, and probably is a reflection of the differences in outlook between head teachers and psychologists. Vernon places perception in a developmental perspective. It depends on the maturation of the sensory apparatus and on the development of linkages of the neurones in the cerebral cortex. Perception involves the ability to recognize "whole units" and also the ability to recognize the details within a whole. This in itself reflects the development of meaningfulness and this can come only from experience. A child does not possess the neurological equipment at birth, or the experience to understand incoming stimuli, either visually or auditorally. This understanding develops with age and is very much dependent on the environment in which the infant is reared. Poor vision and poor hearing are fairly easily recognizable, but difficulty with perception is less so. It can arise from damage to parts of the brain, it can also arise from deficiencies in the environment. P. E. Vernon† has shown that on a variety of cognitive tasks, some of which involve visual perception, West Indian children are seriously impaired in comparison with English children. This is likely to arise from differences in the West Indian culture pattern and physical environment. Evidence

* VERNON, M.D., *Backwardness in Reading*, Cambridge: Cambridge University Press, 1957.
† VERNON, P. E., Environmental handicaps and intellectual development, Part II. *Brit. J. Educ. Psychol.* **35**, 117–26 (1965).

from tests which depend on visual perception shows that perceptual stimuli which are normal in one culture are abnormal in another. It is possible that within different families children are encouraged differentially in the activities that are permissible, thereby leading to differential patterns of appreciation and learning of perceptual clues.

Despite the developmental view of perception, Doman* has developed the idea that even infants can learn to read. His argument is that stimuli need to presented "larger than life" for the child to learn, and in consequence offers printed material drawn very large as a basis for the child's first learning. Whether or not on other grounds this early approach to learning is justified, the evidence he offers seems to support his contention. Perhaps more constructively, he has been able to build up learning programmes for children whose perceptual abilities have been impaired by brain damage, and many of these children have learned to read. It may well be the case that traditionally we have waited for developmental growth to take place instead of helping it to take place by the provision of suitable experience.

Vigotsky† says the same thing in connection with the development of language and thought.

When we study children who have been at school for a number of years, and who have failed in reading, it is difficult to separate out those perceptual difficulties with which a child may have started school and those which have arisen from a failure in learning to read. Goins,‡ however, attempted to relate visual perceptual abilities and development in reading in young children in their first year at school. The children were, on balance, average to superior in intelligence, and some of course had already started to read. She used fourteen different perceptual tests and related scores on them to improvement in reading over a five-month period.

The perceptual abilities which the tests examined were most

† Vigotsky, *op. cit.*
* Doman, *op. cit.*
‡ Goins, J. T., *Visual Perceptual Abilities and Early Reading Progress*, Supplementary Educational Monographs, Chicago: University of Chicago Press, 1958.

satisfactorily explained as involving two different factors, one of which was related to progress in reading, the other was not. The factor related to progress in reading was defined as the ability to "*retain a figure in a distracting field*". The unrelated factor was defined as the ability "*to make a closure* (i.e. make sense) *in an unorganized field*". In other words, the essential perceptual ability depends on seeing and remembering what remains the same, even though the other visual components are changed. This is an interesting finding since it is related to the ideas which Piaget (see Flavell*) has developed in the field of understanding numerical and spatial relationships. He presents the following example. At one stage two identical rows of beads are recognized as being identical only if the rows are matched up one to one. If, however, one row is brought together or extended, whilst retaining the same number of beads, the child will argue that the number of beads is no longer the same in the two rows. When the child is able to retain the figure against a changing field he is said to be able to "conserve" quantities, and therefore to have a more realistic concept of number. The important point is that a visual component retains its identity despite changes in the visual context. Although this may be thought to be merely a function of memory, memory is only a part of the process.

Summing up her work Goins suggests that *in learning to read it is necessary to do two things at the same time: to grasp the wholeness of a visual configuration (e.g. a word) and to be able to analyse the separate parts of that wholeness (e.g. the letters).* Failure in either part of the process is likely to lead to difficulty in reading.

A Psycho-linguistic Approach

More recently McCarthy and Kirk† have developed a model of psycho-linguistic abilities in which the view is taken that the

* FLAVELL, J. H., *The Developmental Psychology of Jean Piaget*, Princeton: D. Van Nostrand, 1963.

† MCCARTHY, J. J. and KIRK, S. A., *Illinois Test of Psycho-linguistic Abilities*, Illinois: University of Illinois, 1961.

individual, if he is to be able to communicate successfully with others, must function in a number of different ways. The underlying assumptions would seem to stem from *information theory*. The model postulates two levels of functioning. The *representational* level involves successively *decoding* or understanding incoming information, *association* or the ability to relate symbols on the basis of their meaning, and *encoding* which is the ability to put meaning into symbols for the benefit of the recipient. Information is received through a number of *channels*, the most important of which are the *visual* and the *auditory*. Information is transmitted primarily through *vocal* and *motor channels*.

The second level is called the *integration* level and involves those processes which tend to become automatic, e.g. the parts of speech, grammar, and various sequential operations. Many motor skills should become consolidated at the integration level.

This model can be used, with certain additions, as a basis for investigating the reading process, and this was done by Kass.* The findings, based on twenty-one seriously retarded children aged 7 years to 10 years, were that these children showed deficiencies in the following areas: the ability to draw meaningful relations from what is heard (Auditory–Vocal Association), the ability to reproduce a series of symbols presented visually (Visual Motor Sequencing), the ability to blend sounds (Vocal Automatic), the ability manually to carry out a visual prediction (Mazes), the ability to reproduce a visual image from memory and the ability to compare detailed visual figures rapidly. Most of these abilities are in fact at the *integration* level rather than at the *representation* level. This is interesting since tests at the *representation* level are in fact more like conventional verbal intelligence tests than are tests at the *integration* level. The important aspect of the approach along psycho-linguistic lines is the fact that the advocates for the use of the model aim to set up teaching programmes to strengthen any weak aspects which an individual is found to have. This is

* KASS, C. E., *Some Psychological Correlates of Severe Reading Disability (Dyslexia) in Selected Studies on the Illinois Test of Psycho-linguistic Abilities*, Madison: Photo Press, 1963.

not to provide "remedial reading" as such, but rather to further those skills which are basic to learning to read.

A point needs to be made about studies such as the one just reported. When we examine a group of children and find deficiencies which are characteristic of the group, we have not in fact found out anything about a single child. It is doubtful if any one child in Kass's sample manifested *all* the weaknesses which he lists. Some may well have shown strength where the others showed weakness. Findings from groups of children are certainly valuable in suggesting further lines of inquiry, but to understand a single child may require a different sort of inquiry. One such inquiry was carried out by Bartlett and Shapiro* and it bears some relationship to the study of Kass.

They were presented with a dull 9-year-old boy who was unable to read and who was reported to show a severe psychiatric disturbance. The theoretical model of learning to read was presented as involving:

  (a) the correct perception of visual, auditory and kinaesthetic (motor) patterns;
  (b) the ability to make the correct connections between the patterns;
  (c) the effective retention of these connections.

The investigation involved setting up experimental conditions whereby the boy could be compared with a control group of comparable age, ability level and reading attainment. It was found that the boy's primary difficulty arose in the early stages of learning the connections between visual and auditory patterns. On subsequent days he was able to re-learn comparatively easily and by the third day he had learned as well as a control subject. After a five-day gap his retention was also as good as that of the control. In other words, he was an abnormally slow learner initially, but what was learned was retained well. The authors

* BARTLETT, D. and SHAPIRO, M. B., Investigation and treatment of a reading disability in a dull child with severe psychiatric disturbances. *Brit. J. Educ. Psychol.* **26,** 180–90 (1956).

were able to introduce a reading programme which took account of the boy's particular difficulty, and progress was subsequently satisfactory.

The great value of this type of study rests on the attempt to study an individual case, using an experimental method based on a rational theoretical model, and with the possibility that the results will have greater generality than the initial problem which was to be investigated might have implied. Conversely, studies of this nature are very time-consuming and it may not be possible to carry them out in any setting except that of hospital with wide resources of time and perhaps manpower for investigation and research.

This chapter has described a number of factors which are related to the dimension involving causes within the child. At the same time all of these factors have been pre-eminently factors which are part of the psychologist's professional framework. There are other "within the child" dimensions which have not been discussed and these will be taken up in subsequent chapters.

CHAPTER 5

Sociological and Family Dimensions

THE second of the dimensions to which head teachers attributed reading failure referred to causes operating within the family. In this chapter we will look at some of these factors. We can recognize a broad set of factors, which are related to social class, and a more specific set of factors which cut across social class, and which may be of more serious significance. This latter set is closely concerned with the dynamics of the relationships between the members of a family, and may therefore be envisaged as a family dimension.

Social Class Factors

Although we are primarily concerned with reading difficulties, it is not always possible to separate out overall low attainment in all school subjects from poor attainment in reading alone. This is especially true when we are concerned with social class. If overall attainment in school is related to social class, then so also is reading attainment. It is necessary, therefore, to examine this relationship and try to understand it.

The publication of the Plowden Report (1967) marks the culmination of a series of studies on the Primary School and primary school children. Of special value is Wiseman's study, which is reported in detail. Wiseman set out to examine the relationships between a wide number of variables in connection with education at the primary stage. These variables included social class status, socio-economic status, and school attainments in a variety of subjects. He submitted his data to detailed statistical analyses. One of his conclusions was that overall attainment in school is most closely related to the *parental attitude to education* and *literacy in the home*. More specifically, if the father is actively and positively concerned about education and his child's school progress, then attainment is likely to be good, and if there is a lack of maternal care for the child, attainment is likely to be poor. Wiseman makes the point that parental occupation and salary are not necessarily major determinants of good overall attainment. He argues that a good salary and a middle-class background are not guarantees of high educational attainment, and that within a poor home, a positive approach to education, a willingness of the parents to read, and a positive maternal attitude to the children will be conducive to good attainment, and unlikely to lead to backwardness.

The detailed study of reading attainments in Kent schools by Morris* needs to be read in conjunction with Wiseman's study. Morris was primarily concerned with reading attainment, and she related this to a wide number of other variables. Her findings are complementary to Wiseman's. She found a high correlation $(0 \cdot 57)$ between social class and reading attainment, a relationship raised to $0 \cdot 68$ if the socio-economic status of schools was related to reading attainment. When she studied poor readers in the sample, she found that fathers were low in occupational status, members of the family showed little interest in reading, mothers had full-time jobs and there was little encouragement at home from the parents. Social class influences are, therefore, clearly of considerable importance in determining the extent to which children master school subjects, reading in particular. It is not enough, however, merely to cite the evidence. It is necessary to try to understand how these influences operate.

We have suggested earlier that the reasons adults provide for learning to read are of doubtful relevance to children. Why then do they learn? Piaget† argues that many of children's

* MORRIS, J. M., *Standards and Progress in Reading*, Slough: N.F.E.R., 1966.
† PIAGET, J., *Play, Imitations and Dreams in Early Childhood*, London: Heinemann, 1951.

activities rest on imitation of others, especially between the ages of 2 years and 7 years. This can be seen very clearly in their play, which is frequently imitative of parental activities. The role of the model, according to Piaget, is extremely important. "To our mind the dynamic link is to be found in compulsion, authority and unilateral respect, *which give rise to imitation of the superior by the subordinate*, or in mutual respect and intellectual or moral equality, *which are the origin of imitation between equals*" (authors' italics). In fact, children imitate what they evaluate positively and they learn by trying to emulate the activities of those people whom they hold in high esteem. The esteem in which significant others, particularly parents, are held provides a basis for imitation which itself is a channel for learning.

In relation to the social class dimension, the studies of Wiseman and Morris show that reading and the possession of books are, to a great extent, irrelevant concerns in many working-class families. The activities of the parents therefore do not include as part of the imitation model the practice of reading and the concern for reading. If, in fact, parents show a declared concern for reading, but do not read themselves, children value what they do rather than what they say. The argument is not that working-class parents in general are opposed to reading, but rather that they are indifferent to it. Under these circumstances, the models to be imitated are more likely to be older children who do read, and enjoy it, or the teachers. Unfortunately recent evidence in this country and in America suggests that many working-class parents prepare their children for school by indicating to the child that the teacher is on the other side of "them and us", and that success in school rests on passivity and compliance. If this is the case, any success of the teacher may depend on her being an authoritarian figure, which itself may serve to inhibit learning unless the authority is benevolent (see Argylle*).

By contrast, in literate middle-class homes, the parents are likely to be seen to enjoy reading. They are likely to demonstrate,

* ARGYLLE, M., *The Psychology of Interpersonal Relationships*, Harmondsworth: Penguin Books, 1967.

in practical activities, their concern for reading, and they are likely to indicate to their children a positive evaluation of the children's own reading. Under these circumstances, many middle-class children will have started to read before going to school and, moreover, their parents will have prepared them to see teachers as an extension of parents, and not as authority figures (Hess and Shipman*). Learning to read, therefore, for middle-class children is likely to be comparatively easy, and accepted as a valued aspect of growing up. The models to be imitated are seen to practise those activities which children need to master for themselves.

Wiseman's findings that maternal care is an important determinant of backwardness and the degree of paternal interest is an important determinant of success can be understood in the light of this analysis. Within working-class families maternal care varies: it can be of the highest or the lowest order. Father's interest can be positive or negative, or neutral. Not all working-class children fail to learn to read. Some learn very well, some very badly. Where reading failure occurs it is likely to stem from the fact that the parental models fail to generate the esteem which is necessary for imitation to take place, and at the same time the activities of those models is unrelated to the learning process, especially reading.

Bernstein† has developed a description of a further dimension which is relevant when we are concerned with social class and learning. This dimension is related to the vocabulary and the structure of the language which is available and which is used in the homes of people of different social classes. Broadly speaking, the language fits into two distinct linguistic codes, described as *restricted* and *elaborate*. The two codes are different in both function and syntax. Whereas the elaborate code is used to signify the individuality of both listener and speaker, the "restricted code" is used to signal the sameness of speaker and listener.

---

* HESS, R. D. and SHIPMAN, V., Early blocks to children's learning. *Children*, **12**, 189–94 (1965).

† BERNSTEIN, B., Language and social class. *Brit. J. Social.* **11**, 271–6 (1960).

In the former case, people are assumed to have different views and, consequently, speech tends to be complex, involving complex sentences with a wide variety of qualifying words (adjectives and adverbs) and qualifying phrases and clauses. In the latter case, the similarities of people's views are taken for granted, and speech tends merely to signal those similarities. Individuality tends to be expressed by tone and gesture. In consequence restricted language tends to involve few qualifiers, to be active in mood as opposed to passive, and to be impersonal.

"Restricted language" is common to all classes and is used in situations where individuality can be taken for granted, e.g. within a family or within a club. "Elaborate language", however, tends to be associated with the middle classes where it is considered important to recognize individuality and where verbal techniques involving explanation are used for social training. The language to be found in books, certainly at more advanced levels than the first early readers, tends to be "elaborate" rather than "restricted". Thus the child of working-class families is confronted at school with a linguistic code with which he is unfamiliar at home, and which in many ways fails to convey the sorts of meaning with which he is acquainted. The impact of this is likely to be felt more intensely at the secondary level where books may be used to convey information as opposed to providing merely a narrative.

An example may help to clarify the problem. A 14-year-old boy attended the child guidance clinic for help with his reading, which was at about the 8-year level. He made fair but slow progress, to some extent because correspondence and articles in one of the tabloid papers was used. On one occasion, however, he was reading from a book geared to the older backward reader and was confronted with the following sentence: "Tugboat Annie was liked by all the people in the docks." He got as far as the word "was" and then stopped with a puzzled look. The sentence was rewritten, "All the people in the docks liked Tugboat Annie", and this he read unhesitatingly. He was asked about the difficulty and his reply was to the effect that the word "liked" in the original sentence did not seem to make sense, so he did not go on. Using the idea of different linguistic codes, we can say that the sentence in its first form was using elaborate language, expressing an idea using the passive mood. The idea presented in the second form used the active mood, form which is more common in the restricted code. For this boy it was not that the words could not be read, but that the linguistic form, and therefore the thought form, was unusual. This effectively inhibited the boy's ability to read the particular sentence.

Middle-class children are not confronted with this particular difficulty to the extent that working-class children are. The consequence will be that reading may be inhibited for the child from a working-class family by virtue of the unexpected complexity of the language in the printed word. It may lead to reading itself becoming for the child a boring, because unmeaningful, activity, and it may be to a great extent responsible for the loss of interest in reading by boys and girls when they have left school.

Intra-family Dimensions

Whereas the sociological dimensions are likely to be related to large numbers of children within the working classes, the intra-family dimension is likely to affect very few families, but to be responsible for some of the very severe reading disabilities. The basic model for this approach stems from social psychology and psychiatry, and involves examining the roles of the husband and wife at the time of marriage, and after the advent of children in the family. A full account is given by Miller and Westman.*

It is assumed that all people have certain needs which can be either recognized or unrecognized, and that these are met by forming relationships with other people. Marriage may be one such relationship. The needs are recognized by the way in which they play out certain roles within the family in contrast with their

---

* MILLER, D. R. and WESTMAN, J. C., Reading disability as a condition of family stability. *Fam. Proc.* **3**, 66–76. (1964); Family teamwork and psychotherapy. *Fam. Proc.* **4**, 49–56. (1965)

behaviour in the outer world. Where a marriage relationship is based on unrecognized needs, the role lived out at home tends to be radically different from that lived out in the world at large. Where these differences occur the marriage itself may contain many tensions, but, because the needs are unrecognized, they cannot be dealt with by verbalization and discussion. The partners become locked then in a relationship which is very stable and, at the same time, inflexible. Frequently the partners have themselves suffered serious emotional damage as children.

When children are born, the marital partners should develop new roles as parents, which means also new roles in relation to each other. But because the marriage is both stable and inflexible, the development of new roles provides a threat to the existing relationship. To reduce the threat the infant never becomes an individual in his own right, but becomes a tool for the parents to use in order to maintain the *status quo*. Part of the process can be the keeping of the growing child as the baby, or as the stupid one in the family.

Miller and Westman studied the families of eighteen children who had failed to benefit from any form of remedial help in reading. They were seriously retarded, yet they were found to be of average or higher intelligence, free from physical or physiological handicap and not seriously mentally ill. These children had been referred to hospital for help with reading problems. All the families of this group of children fell into the pattern which has been described above. Among the parents, many had had reading difficulties at school, and in some instances the father was on the borderline of severe mental illness.

One characteristic of these families was that although they wanted their children to read, their attempts at help continued to militate against any success. Either they demanded an inappropriately high level of performance which made progress impossible, or they used severe and humiliating punishment for failure. This, of course, was an effective way of maintaining the role of the child as the stupid one. It also happened frequently that, despite the presenting problem about the child's not reading, the parents would then ask for help because of some other behaviour such as the child's being a nuisance. It is not surprising that these parents were reluctant to look more deeply at the problems of their own marriage relationships and at the same time tended to sabotage any help that might be given for the children's reading difficulties, although this was what had been asked for. When a child did make progress one of the parents might show signs of becoming mentally ill.

Each child in the group seemed to present himself in three different identities or roles which the authors describe in the following way. "One (identity) might be described as a frightened, cautious, daydreaming, asexual and stupid baby, the second as an omnipotent, manipulating, dominant, needling and sadistic adolescent, the third as a socially bright, confident but overburdened, premature adult." There is a striking similarity between this analysis and the type of analysis given by Berne,* where he describes the transactions which take place between people, and the transactional games that they play. An essential characteristic of his model is the recognition of identities which an individual may show. One identity typifies a parent, one typifies an adult and one typifies a child. There is also a similarity between Miller and Westman investigations and those which relate schizophrenia to the roles which parents live out between each other, at the cost of the mental health of one or more of the children.

Miller, in a personal communication, suggests that perhaps as many as 15% of severely retarded readers fall into the pattern which he has described. Whilst his cases are derived from families which are recognized as being severely disturbed, it may well be the case that many children suffer from milder degrees of this kind of disturbance in a wide range of families.

This theoretical explanation of reading difficulty in relation to family interactions is comparatively new and consequently the known cases which fit the model are as yet comparatively rare. The likelihood is that many children whose reading difficulty has been described in other terms would just as well have fitted into

* BERNE, E., *Games People Play*, New York: Grove Press, 1964.

the group where the handicap could be considered to have origin-
ated from the adaptation to the role cast for the child by disturbed
parents. In particular, many children who are labelled "dyslexic"
(see Chapter 7) may well fit this pattern. Miller suggests that the
handicap seems to be handed down from father to son, a condition
which is frequently described as "hereditary". "Heredity" is
frequently postulated as the basis for "dyslexia".

CHAPTER 6

Dimensions within the School Setting—Staffing, Materials and Methods

THE third set of factors which were considered by head teachers to be related to reading difficulty stemmed from the school itself. Many children seem able to acquire at least the beginnings of reading without any help from the school, but less able children are frequently entirely dependent on the school for the beginnings and development of reading skill. And those who have made a start need the continued help and guidance that the school has to offer. The school, therefore, must be considered to be the place where learning to read is of primary importance—especially the infant school. It is unfortunately not always recognized how important the infant school is.

A number of factors which can foster or hinder the learning process can be separated out for comment. In the first place, the classroom needs to be provided with materials which will be conducive to learning to read. Children will not be interested unless colourful books and pictures are a regular feature of the environment. These things, of course, can be too attractive in the sense that pictures which are too easily understandable may obviate the need to learn to read. In other words, there must be a balance between those stimuli which carry their own immediate satisfactions, and are complete in themselves, and those which lead the child to read the printed word. But above all, the material must be recognized as meaningful to the child, and relevant to his interests and what he wants to do. The provision of such materials will very much depend on the financial resources which are available to a head teacher, and also on the educational strategies which the head teacher wishes to pursue within the school.

A second factor is that what is to be learned must be related to the child's level of development and the area of his interests. The novels of Dickens would not be suitable reading material for infant-age children, although some of his narratives might conceivably be suitable for reading aloud to very young children. There must be some correspondence between where a child is and where he is expected to go. If this is not present there is a serious danger that the child will either actively retreat from or passively resist the learning process. Much has been said of "reading readiness", but it is doubtful if it is sufficiently well defined a concept to have much value. Doman* has already been able to show that infants can learn to read if the material is presented by the right person in the right way. Downing† has critically discussed "reading readiness" and suggests that we need to retain some such concept so long as we recognize that "reading readiness" hinges very much on the situation and the people who will teach, whether parents or teachers. There is a serious danger that in using a concept such as "reading readiness" we assume that we have to *wait* until the child is ready. This is useful if we wish to protect children from too severe a pressure to learn, but it is harmful if it implies that the child cannot be helped to become ready to read by providing suitable experience. Vigotsky‡ was very much aware of this danger, and recognized that it was more important to find out what the child could do with adult help rather than to wait absolutely for the child to indicate that he was ready. Vigotsky called this the area of potential development and it is unfortunate that his work has been relatively inaccessible in English translation until fairly recently. The application of Vigotsky's formulation must lead

* DOMAN, G. J., *Teach your Baby to Read*, London: Cape, 1965.

† DOWNING, J., Reading Readiness Re-assessed, in *The First International Reading Symposium, Oxford, 1964*, London: Cassell, 1966.

‡ VIGOTSKY, L. S., *Thought and Language*, Massachusetts: M.I.T. 1st) English translation), 1962.

to more active teaching whereas the waiting for readiness may lead to passive attitudes in teaching methods.

The third factor is concerned more with teachers themselves. To teach children to read is highly skilled activity, especially for the average and below-average child. It should be the case, therefore, that all teachers in infant schools, and many in junior and secondary schools, should be trained in the teaching of reading. It is known, however, that in many areas there may be as many as 30% of the teachers who are completely unqualified, and of the 70% who are technically qualified many have not undergone professional training at all or, if they have, were not taught the teaching of reading. Thus in such areas, usually working-class areas, the professional help that is needed for teaching children to read is in very short supply. It is not surprising that many children have difficulty with reading when their teaching is in the hands of unqualified teachers.

The fourth factor (and this is closely related to the third) hinges on the stability of staff over time. Children need constancy in their environment, especially in the infant school. Ideally the staff should remain relatively unchanged for most of the child's infant school life. Teachers are important for children, but only if they are there long enough for the child to understand the teacher and the teacher to understand the child. But in working-class areas, where staffing is extremely difficult, half of the staff within a single school may leave in one year and be replaced only in part. There is no permanent core to the staff except perhaps for the head teacher and the deputy head teacher. The child has no consistent or enduring adults for him either to identify himself with, or for them to be able to pace his temporal development. The child measures his own development by the relatively unchanging nature of the teachers. But if these frequently change he is bound to be confused. Under these circumstances, the learning process, especially in the basic subjects, will be hindered.

Another consequence of this rapid staff turnover is that the head teacher cannot plan an educational programme which he or she knows will be implemented. Thus teaching methods fail to be consistently applied and long-term planning for the provision of educational materials, e.g. books and reading schemes, runs the risk of being an academic exercise unrelated to reality. Once again, many children will not receive the most appropriate conditions for learning to read.

These factors are relatively independent of teaching methods as such, and each, in turn, will affect the general standards of reading attainment within a school and together they will have an even greater affect on children who may be especially liable to reading failure. It is unfortunately the case that the various factors will tend to work together where schools and children are in depressed and deprived areas, so that in these areas children's reading difficulties are likely to be accentuated. The details of teaching methods, however, are also of considerable importance and need to be looked at separately.

Teaching Methods

The adoption of different teaching methods tends to go in phases of action and reaction, governed more by fashion than by research and evaluation (cf. Young*). The history of reading methods has been very well described by Diack† and he remarks that although there have been two major approaches to the teaching of reading, i.e. through visual and phonic methods, the actual content of the different methods have borne little relationship to the names which the methods carry.

The broad difference in methods is based primarily on a dichotomy between the recognition of meaningful "wholes", e.g. sentences or words, and the learning of the constituent parts of the wholes, i.e. letters, which separately are relatively meaningless. Thus we have the "look and say" method, and the "phonic" method or, more correctly, groups of methods. Usually these methods are set in opposition, probably because each set of

---

* YOUNG, M., *Innovation and Research in Education*, London: Routledge & Kegan Paul, 1965.

† DIACK, H., *In Spite of the Alphabet*, London: Chatto & Windus, 1965.

methods lends itself to gross distortion. "Look and say" frequently leads to "look and guess" or just "guess" (Webster*) and phonic methods frequently lead to the meaningless repetition of meaningless letter sounds and subsequently meaningless sentences.

Certain basic issues, however, must be considered in relation to the teaching methods which are used. We can distinguish between the complexity of the visual symbol which has to be related to a particular sound and the meaningfulness whereby the symbol represents a mental process. As an example, the word "aeroplane" is meaningful and visually complex, the word "mat" is both meaningful and visually less complex, the letter "a" is relatively meaningless and visually very simple. It is usually the case that meaningfulness and visual complexity go together. It is also true that children need meaningfulness in order to gain their interest. This is the cornerstone of the "look and say" set of methods. We shall take up some of the problems of this approach a little later.

Whilst it is undoubtedly true that meaning is important, other aspects of the reading skill are equally important. Words are made up of constituent letters, and these provide the essential tools for learning to read words that have not previously been known. It is necessary, therefore, for the child to become acquainted with letters and their sounds in order to be independent of the teacher in dealing with new words. At the same time an even more important principle is involved. Letters and words only have the correct informational content if they are read from left to right, and the ability to cope with this skill in organizing the sequences may have to be learned. It cannot be learned purely from the recognition of a word shape. The phonic approach emphasizes this left to right orientation as well as dealing with letter sounds. The price, however, which may have to be paid rests in the fact that the English language spelling is not entirely simple nor straightforward. Although there are rules, the exceptions are so frequent

* WEBSTER, J., *Practical Reading: Some New Remedial Techniques*, London: Evans, 1965.

that they limit the meaningful aspect of sequences of words which are easily readable in a purely phonetical manner.

We can now turn separately to some of the main difficulties which stem from the two contrasted approaches. "Look and say" systems involve an associative learning process, i.e. picture goes with visual symbol linked with sounds which are words. As a result of a number of repetitions in a variety of contexts the child associates a meaningful picture, with its word attached, with an initially meaningless visual array of symbols, i.e. letters. It is held that the child becomes familiar with the shape of the word and eventually "knows" that shape to be a word. Webster (*op. cit.*) argues very properly that this method is basically inefficient, since a time gap occurs between looking at the picture which represents an object and looking at the word placed under the picture. Ideally both should be seen at the same time for learning to occur, but since learning should be of the word, not of the picture, the sequence should be first the word on its own, then word and picture simultaneously (and here the picture merely provides a cue), then the word on its own again. Webster has developed techniques which, in effect, represent a new method of teaching reading and which meet this requirement.

Clearly, for a child to learn by the recognized "look and say" method he must have a good short-term memory capacity, and be able to take in perceptually a quite complex visual stimulus. It is very doubtful if, in fact, children do learn the "shapes" of words. It is more likely that they recognize the word by some small peculiarity, e.g. one or two letters, often the first or last. If this is the case, Webster is right in suggesting that the method leads to guessing rather than to genuine recognition and learning. Learning probably comes indirectly from a process of the child's recognition of some similarities and differences between different words, and then developing his own rules for working out the correct sound. This process of finding similarities and differences is basically an intellective skill, and it probably underlies much of the relationship between intelligence and reading attainment that was discussed in Chapter 4. By the same reasoning it seems that the bright children would be less likely to be hindered by a "look and say" approach to reading than those of lower intelligence.

Another disadvantage of the "look and say" method is that since children can always guess the word there is no feed back available to correct errors unless the teacher is always on hand. Once the habit of guessing without correction is acquired it is extremely difficult subsequently to build in corrective experience. The child therefore is almost encouraged to mislearn, and, in a way, discouraged from correcting mistakes in learning. It is not difficult to recognize the child with reading difficulties who has been taught by visual methods. It is as though he has learned the beginnings and ends of words in a positive way, and in a negative way has learned that the middles of words have no discriminatory value.

The phonic method on its part also has serious disadvantages. The method rests on the premise that words can be built up from their constituent parts, i.e. letters. If the sounds are known, then the word can be created. This is true, however, only for words which obey phonetic rules, and unfortunately very many words defy these rules. To attempt to read the word "enough" phonetically is to end up with nonsense. Thus the knowledge of sounds as represented by letters cannot carry the pupil all the way, although it may carry him a part of the way. There is also a fallacy in thinking that each letter carries a discrete sound. It is usually the case that any letter derives its sound value from the letters which precede or succeed it within a word. In fact it is almost impossible not to make two sounds out of a consonant instead of one, e.g. "c" as in "cat" usually becomes "k(er)", which, of course, is more than the child needs. In consequence, when a child builds up a word phonetically he creates a sound which is incorrect, e.g. "k(er)at(er)" for *cat*. In practice he uses the stimulus of the sound that he makes to guess in accordance with his experience of what the word is likely to be. The phonetic reader may guess just as much as the "look and say" reader. If the child is lucky he may be able to get the correct sound from the context of the passage. This near impossibility of reproducing sounds correctly can sometimes be overcome by learning to blend the sounds of two or more adjacent letters and here we are almost back at the practice of visual recognition of unit wholes. The difference lies in the fact that in word blending the cue is through auditory channels, in word recognition the cue is provided through visual channels.

It is interesting that the elements of teaching which are emphasized in either of these methods come in at the back door, as it were, in the other method. Each method utilizes a vital aspect of the reading process and tends to ignore other aspects. Children, however, are frequently able to bring about a balance out of necessity and through the development and use of intellectual strategies. It is unfortunate that the visual and phonic methods are so frequently set in opposition since the differences are reconcilable. Differences in the visual complexity of the basic units of reading which typify the "visual" and the "phonic" approaches are only a matter of degree. Visual methods are supposed to foster interest because the material used has meaning, but it could be asked how much difference there is between the early "look and say" books and the early "phonic" books. In fact each type is equally dull. The problem with each lies in its one-sidedness. The result is that some children must suffer. Children vary in the extent to which they can cope with visual complexity. They vary in their preference for a visual or an auditory approach. They vary in the extent to which they have the native wit to compensate for the failures in the methods by which they are taught. They vary in the extent to which they can tolerate the repetitive material in the first books they are expected to read. Either set of methods therefore can contribute to reading failure.

These two methods utilize respectively the visual and the auditory sensory channels. There are, however, two other modalities which are available as channels for learning. They are the kinaesthetic (or motor) and the tactile (or touch) modalities. The only method which stresses the former is that developed by Fernald*

---

* FERNALD, G. M., *Remedial Techniques in Basic School Subjects*, New York: McGraw-Hill, 1943.

in which the basic learning arises from carrying out writing movements which match in some way with sounds. The method is frequently used with seriously retarded children and often is the only method which shows results with children who are gravely disturbed. The practical disadvantage of this method is that it can only be carried out where classes are very small, and even then preferably where there is a one-to-one ratio of staff to pupils.

Moxon* developed a system of remedial reading which involved two principles. The first principle was that the child should be active in his approach to reading and he achieved this by so arranging the classroom that the child actually did something in order to get information which he needed, e.g. he had to lift a flap to find the letter sound of the letter on the flap. The second principle involved the deliberate and active analysis of words prior to reading them. Any word that the child did not know had to be reproduced with letters printed on 1-inch squares of cardboard. The reconstituted words were placed into slots which allowed for isolating successively first the vowel, then the vowel and the end letter, and finally the whole of a syllable. Letter sounds which were not known could be found from appropriate charts. In this way analysis and synthesis were carried out by the child almost without his knowing it. Kinaesthesis was used in this method, not in connection with individual letters, but as part of the process of analysis. The method has the great advantage of placing the emphasis on the printed word and not on cues that might lead to recognition without learning. Elkonin† in Russia developed a comparable thesis based on Pavlovian theory. The argument is that analysis may have to be taught as a process, and therefore the analytic process must be worked out in detail in order that the child can learn.

It is surprising that the role of kinaesthetic and tactile learning should have received such limited attraction in this country since

* MOXON, C. A. V., *A Remedial Teaching Method*, London: Methuen, 1962.

† ELKONIN, D. B., *The Psychology of Mastering the Elements of Reading in Educational Psychology in the U.S.S.R.*, London: Routledge & Kegan Paul, 1963.

the infant's earliest and often the most stable learning comes from movement and touch (cf. Piaget*). These modalities are not, of course, ignored in the ordinary process of learning. Children learn to write at the same time as learning to read, and their educational material usually allows for tactile learning. It would seem, however, that neither modality has received separate consideration as a basic channel for learning. No single method, in fact, has been devised which can take advantage of all the child's sense modalities. Those aspects of the learning process that are ignored in a teaching method inevitably are used by children in a haphazard manner. This does not lead to efficient learning.

The final consideration in this chapter must be some mention of the Initial Teaching Alphabet (i.t.a.). English spelling presents a number of problems because of its many irregularities. Although head teachers did not give this as a reason for reading failure, theorists have for many years argued that spelling should be systematized. The solution to the problem which i.t.a. offers is the creation of extra letters to the existing alphabet so that it is possible to create a one-to-one correspondence between letter and sound. The complete i.t.a. is given in Fig. 1 and it can be seen that the new letters show some visual correspondence with the combinations of letters which they replace.

The aim of this correspondence is in order to allow for transfer to the use of traditional orthography at a later stage.

The evidence so far available (Downing†) is certainly consistent with the notion that reading skill can be helped considerably if children learn first in i.t.a., but there has been considerable controversy as to what the improvement is really due to. Is it a case of any new technique producing improvement or the singling out of certain groups of children for special methods? Are the teachers who use i.t.a. more enlightened or progressive than other teachers?

* PIAGET, J., *The Psychology of Intelligence*, London: Routledge & Kegan Paul, 1950.

† DOWNING, J., The Initial Teaching Alphabet, in *The First International Reading Symposium, Oxford, 1964*, London: Cassell, 1966.

Pitman's i.t.a. ('Monotype' Ehrhardt Series 453)

REGD. TRADE MARK
MONOTYPE

SYNOPSIS OF CHARACTERS

æbcdɛefghiejklmnœprɪrstuevwyzʒʍhɥhchthʃhʃhʒŋaɑauenouɷɷouoi
1234567890   ´   .,·:!?

THE MAJUSCULE ALPHABET, FIGURES AND POINTS SHOWN ABOVE ARE SERIES L211

æbcdɛefghiejklmnœprɪrstuevwyzʒʍhɥhchthʃhʃhʒŋaɑauenouɷɷouoi
1234567890 F1092   .,·;!?·'()-

THE MINUSCULE ALPHABET CONSISTS OF STANDARD LETTERS FROM SERIES 453 WITH THE ADDITION OF THE FOLLOWING SPECIAL LETTERS

d	ɛɛ	f	g	ie	r	ue	ɴ	wh	ɥ	th	th	ʃh	ʒ	ŋ	a	au	ɑ	ŋ	ɷ	ɷ	ou	oi
784 d	1905 e	457 f	655 g	163 i	732 r	971 u	559 z	283 w	676 t	675 t	680 c	905 s	118 z	623 n	2420 a	2027 a	1874 a	623 n	1599 o	1600 o	258 o	1553 o

12 PT. (12D) 11 SET   LINE M·1381

ſhe kwick broun foks jumps œver the læʒy dog. but chil̶dren hœ lern
tœ reeɖ ɸhrœ i.t.a. with its raʃhonal spelliŋ enjoi reeɖiŋ and aull ſhær
lievs afterwaurɖʒ ar æbl tœ pœt this luv ov bœks tœ gœd ues,
whether for pleʒuer or·study.

FIG. 1. The Initial Teaching Alphabet.

It is doubtful if these questions will ever be satisfactorily answered to meet all critics, but perhaps the more important question to ask is which children continue to fail even with the best of teachers, in the best of circumstances, and when the most simplified orthography available. It must be remembered that *i.t.a.* is a medium through which the spoken word is reduced to visual symbols. It is not a teaching method. Consequently if *i.t.a.* is used, the basic teaching methods, visual, phonic, Fernald, etc., continue to be necessary. Failures due to methods will not be solved merely by changing the medium. It is most unlikely that any one method will ever be found by which reading achievement can be guaranteed. Perhaps the best we can hope for is that innovations of method will be matched by evaluative research rather than merely reflect the change of fashion. And certainly the advocates of the *i.t.a.* have attempted to do just this.

CHAPTER 7

Dyslexia—the Neurological Dimension

WHEREAS the previous chapters have been largely expositional, this chapter inevitably deals with a more controversial issue. The label "dyslexia", or perhaps more popularly "word blindness", has been in use for a period of some seventy years. As early as 1878 Kussmaul used the term "word-blindness" to describe a condition in which people who had no visual defects and were not intellectually below average were unable to read. Since then the condition has been documented in a number of medical publications and the first major authority is probably Hinshelwood* and the most detailed study is by Hallgren,† who related the condition to genetic factors. The current label is "dyslexia", "congenital dyslexia" or "specific developmental dyslexia", and the major exponents of the condition are neurologists.

A number of points need to be raised which will receive considerable amplification in the body of the chapter. Is it fair to ask if the term "dyslexia" implies anything other than an inability to read? Is it a diagnosis or is it merely a descriptive label? The term "haemorrhage" merely means "bleeding". It has no diagnostic significance unless it can be related to causative factors, to location of bleeding and to the implications of bleeding. Is the term dyslexia in the same category?

Dyslexia is related by then eurologists to malfunctioning, in

---

* HINSHELWOOD, J., *Congenital Word Blindness*, London: H. K. Lewis, 1917.

† HALLGREN, B., Specific dyslexia. *Acta Psychiat. Neurol.*, Suppl. 65, 1950.

some ways, of the brain. Is there evidence of structural abnormality to justify that relationship? Without that evidence, structural abnormality can only be a hypothesis, and it can only be of pragmatic value as a hypothesis if it leads to practical procedures. Moreover, such a hypothesis should not be invoked unless all other explanations have been explored and found to be inadequate.

Again it must be asked to what extent neurologists restrict their use of the label to a minority of those cases in which children have a reading disability. Are all cases "dyslexic"? If not, how is the reading disability of the others explained? Are there alternative explanations which neurologists have available for reading disability? Or is the symptom of reading disability the only basis for describing a child as dyslexic? In other words, what conditions of reading disability are excluded by the label "dyslexia"?

In view of these underlying questions, it is not surprising that there is no unanimity of agreement between the different professions who are concerned with reading disability. In particular, the neurologists and the psychologists represent opposed attitudes as to whether or not the condition even exists. Moreover, the press has played a part in publicizing the concept of dyslexia, usually following the lead of the neurologists. In consequence the public has become aware of the issue, without necessarily having any basis for understanding that nature of the issue. The aim of this chapter is to suggest some answers to the questions that have been presented, and at the same time to suggest ways in which the controversy has come about.

If a parent takes a child to a general practitioner complaining that her child, although seemingly intelligent, is unable to read, the doctor is presented with a very real problem. He knows that his training does not include a knowledge of learning processes but he is aware that such matters are possibly related to the malfunctioning of the brain. Consequently he is likely to refer the child to a brain specialist at a hospital. The brain specialist is also not trained in problems of learning, but he does know about how the brain functions, and it is not surprising that he should seek explanations in terms of brain function, especially brain damage. The keen neurologist will probably seek to develop general theories about reading skill in connection with brain function or brain dysfunction. He may also extend his knowledge of brain functioning at the same time. This development provides an example of the way the individual assimilates new information into his existing theories or schemes and modifies them in the light of new knowledge. According to Piaget,* this twin process of assimilation and accommodation is the essence of intellectual growth. This is positive development. There is the risk, however, that, having created one system of explanations which make good sense, this system is used to cover all other cases where, in fact, different dimensions may be more relevant. It may be the case that something of this negative development underlies the controversy about dyslexia from the standpoint of both neurologists and psychologists.

Before attempting a description of what is referred to under the name of dyslexia it needs to be remarked that when the condition was first described the methods of teaching reading in the schools were probably very different from those used at the present time. Since children would not be referred to the hospital for reading failure before they had been subjected to some years of teaching, the neurologist's findings may have been influenced by the inadequacies of the teaching methods previously employed. Even now, when "dyslexia" cases are reported upon, the history of the teaching methods which have been employed are rarely noted, although these teaching methods might throw light on the reading failure. Not infrequently, what the neurologist expects the child to know, e.g. the alphabetic order of the letters, may be unrelated to current educational practice.

The descriptions of "word blindness" which follow are all derived from a conference held under the auspices of the Invalid

* PIAGET, J., *The Psychology of Intelligence*, London: Routledge & Kegan Paul, 1950.

Children's Aid Association (1962).† The conference was arranged in order to draw attention to the problem of "word blindness" and, if possible, to initiate some action. Five exponents of the concept presented material either in formal papers or in discussion, and we have attempted to extract views on "word blindness" from these papers.

Gallagher recognizes a number of categories of reading disability but restricts the use of the term "word blindness" to those individuals whose reading and spelling abilities include bizarre features as well as being limited. Demonstrable brain damage and specific emotional disorders which might precede the condition must be excluded for the diagnosis to be made. How all these conditions can be met is difficult to see. Gallagher's explanatory hypothesis is that account must be taken of "physiological individuality", but the nature of this "individuality" is not easily discoverable by ordinary methods. Word-blind individuals may well have better than average ability and may be able to do mathematics well.

MacDonald Critchley is more specific in his description of the condition. He looks for inadequacies of visual motor abilities together with a history of general clumsiness which tends to be grown out of rather early. Spatial relationships, especially those involving direction orientations, present problems and the understanding of complex visual stimuli provide difficulties. Body-image concepts are impaired and the child has difficulty in handling concepts of time. His explanatory principle is that whereas in most individuals the two halves of the brain develop differentially there is a strong tendency with these children for this differentiation to be delayed or not to take place. The outcome is called "mixed cerebral dominance". Psychologists have frequently sought to relate reading failure to this condition and the results of their inquiries have usually been equivocal. In contrast to Gallagher, Critchley argues that with many of these children arithmetical ability is also impaired.

† I.C.A.A., *Word Blindness or Specific Developmental Dyslexia* (ed. A. W. FRANKLIN), London: Pitman Medical Press, 1962.

Shankweiler attempts to set some limits to the condition by asking a number of specific questions. First, he quite clearly separates the condition from those which include inadequacies of speech and language, and says that it refers to difficulties specific to the production and interpretation of written symbols. Secondly, he restricts the dimensions of these difficulties by excluding failure to identify pictures of objects. Thirdly, the difficulty with words is not paralleled by difficulty in recognition of letters. Fourthly, inversion of letters need not be a feature and he argues that manifest spatial difficulties are not essential to the condition of "dyslexia". Fifthly, memory span for a sequence of symbols is frequently very good. Sixthly, he distinguishes between two conditions, one in which recognition of a word can be made correctly but after a long time, and the other in which this recognition is faulty but the response is given in a short time.

This latter account is remarkable since it seems to challenge everything that everyone else has said, and it seems to make sense only if all retarded children are labelled "dyslexic". If this is the case it is not surprising that the concept of dyslexia is defined away by Shankweiler's specifications.

Worster-Drought relates dyslexia and speech defects together with high intelligence. He, too, argues that attainment in all other school subjects is usually normal, but mirror writing and some disorder in perception of spatial relationships is frequent.

Rheinhold defines the condition as being broadly an inborn deficit giving rise to difficulty in reading, spelling, and to a greater or lesser degree, in right/left orientation occurring in children who are otherwise normal. It may not, however, manifest itself until reading and spelling become more complex than the simple material to be learned at an early level. For Rheinhold also attainment in other subjects is satisfactory. The underlying cause is held to be differences in the brain of the "dyslexic" child, but the disability is primarily one of spelling and only secondarily of reading.

With all this variety, and contradictory statements of definition, it is not surprising that psychologists and neurologists have been unable to find a common ground. The arguments put forward by psychologists need to be examined.

In the first place, most of the criteria held to be typical of "dyslexia" are commonly found in children who either *can* or *cannot* read. Some of these conditions are in any case developmental problems which can be helped by appropriate teaching. Secondly, the diagnostic techniques which neurologists use in their testing of reading ability are usually unstandardized and may be related only to the neurologist's own recollection of his learning experience in school, which is now outmoded. We have already quoted the use of knowledge of the alphabet as a diagnostic cue. Diagnosis which is made on the basis of unstandardized techniques based on outmoded practice is hardly likely to be held as being beyond reproach. Over and above this, the exponents of "dyslexia" seem unable to provide reliable measures of its incidence. Such research as does exist leads to the view that the condition must be extremely rare. Morris,* reporting an extensive study of good and poor readers in Kent, states emphatically that "if 'word-blindness' exists as a condition which cannot be treated by good teaching within the state educational system, it must be a rare condition indeed". Yet one of the points that is usually made about "word blindness" is that it is a condition which is highly intract-able and justifies the provision of special remedial centres.

Educational psychologists prefer to see reading retardation as an extending over a continuum from mild retardation to severe, and they do not see it necessary to postulate a separate group over and above this continuum. One of the great dangers in creating such a group, and giving it a technical label, is that it may allow any child with reading difficulties to be considered as suffering from an intractable condition requiring highly special-ized techniques. Two examples may perhaps illustrate the problem. Two boys had been labelled "dyslexic" by the neurologists and permission was requested for these boys to attend a special unit

* MORRIS, J. M., *Standards and Progress in Reading*, Slough: N.F.E.R., 1966.

each afternoon. The parent of one boy refused but allowed the boy to attend an ordinary remedial centre in his own school. The other boy did attend the special unit, but by the time he started to attend his reading was within the normal limits for his level of ability. He had already been attending an ordinary remedial centre. In fact, both boys made about five years' progress in about two terms. According to the diagnosis, these boys needed special teaching; what they got, in fact, was not *direct* teaching at all. The two different remedial teachers provided an environment in which reading materials were available and left the boys to their own devices. They learned to read. This, of course, showed a high level of professional skill in the teachers, in that they recognized that to apply any pressure, or to set any expectations in connecting with reading, would be self-defeating. This was a valid approach although it hardly made sense in terms of neurological diagnosis. In retrospect it is much more likely that an analysis of the reading difficulty need not have been made within physiological terms and some other system of explanations would have been more appropriate.

In view of the fact that such a controversy exists between psychologists and neurologists it is necessary to try to understand how this has come about. The first point to be made is that the sample which is seen by neurologists is probably very different from that seen by psychologists within the schools system. In the early days it is likely that the neurologically studied sample came from middle-class parents with children attending middle-class schools, probably private schools. No evidence has ever been presented to indicate the social class and educational status of the hospital sample, although repeatedly there is an emphasis that these children are above average intelligence. The sample which is seen by educational psychologists can include the whole gamut of social class and schools systems. It may well also be the case that children seen by one will certainly not be seen by the other. Where the educational psychologist in a local authority and a neurologist in a hospital are both involved with the same individuals the diagnoses are seldom in agreement. The second point arises from the wide variety of descriptions given to the condition "dyslexia". Different neurologists see different samples according to the area in which they work, and according to their special interests. Worster-Drought, for instance, specializes in problems of language and speech disabilities and so it is not surprising that he sees such problems related to "dyslexia". The one attribute common to all neurologists is their training in neurology, and consequently, despite the differences in precise formulation, there are some common features of the condition which lend themselves to physiological rather than to anatomical explanations. Brain damage is usually excluded as an explanation since no evidence for this can be found in physical signs other than the reading failure itself. Thus the definitions of "dyslexia" seem to be variations on a physiological theme, each variation being composed by a different specialist. The theme itself must be deduced from the variations. The third point arises from the fact that, once a category is defined, cases are included into that category on only the merest shred of evidence or without evidence at all apart from the symptom purely for want of alternative explanations. Experience suggests that once a child is seen by a neurologist the "diagnosis" is likely to be "dyslexia". But is not this a verbal description masquerading as diagnosis? It should be remembered that the condition "developmental dyslexia" is supposed to be very rare. It would be interesting to know what percentage of hospital referrals are so described, and what percentage of reading difficulties are given any alternative diagnosis. Much, of course, depends on the way all the evidence is evaluated. It may be difficult for a neurologist to evaluate social and family factors just as it may be difficult for a psychologist to evaluate any neurological factors. If there are only a few ways of formulating a problem, all cases must fit those few ways. And, of course, once a syndrome or condition is created it carries a high professional and emotional involvement which is a serious hindrance to change. This argument applies both to those who formulate a problem in a new way as well as to those who deny the validity of that formulation.

By way of conclusion mention must be made of Ingram's writings.* Ingram is concerned about the dyslexic child, but for him "Dyslexia *is* difficulty in reading, or learning to read". Specific dyslexia refers to only a small minority of the general category of dyslexics. Specific dyslexia comprises a brain-damaged group and a group with no history of, nor clinical findings of, brain damage. The non-brain-damaged group may or may not have a history of speech defects or reading or writing difficulty, but ambidextrality and left-handedness may be important. These definitions are, of course, couched in neurological terms, and seem to embrace a very wide range of children. This analysis, of course, falls within the traditional neurological dimensions and is open to criticism as a set of explanations. But Ingram goes one step further and presents an analysis of specific disabilities which may affect reading. He argues for three areas of disability involving (1) visuo-spatial, (2) correlating (association) and (3) speech-sound difficulties. Each area is broken down into separate reading and writing aspects and within each of these specific difficulties of orientation, recognition, reproduction, analysis and comprehension. The value of this analysis is that it provides a workable frame of reference to which both neurologists and psychologists could subscribe. It sets out an operational scheme which is amenable to research by both parties to the controversy, and should such research be carried out as a twin project, there would be a chance for the controversy about dyslexia to generate fruitful work in the understanding of reading disability. Not only would we know more about reading difficulty but neurologists might also find some insights into the less-well-known aspects of brain and neural functioning. The controversy as it stands is futile. It needs to be dropped and a fresh beginning made.

* INGRAM, T. T. S., The dyslexic child. *The Practitioner: Symposium on the Handicapped Child*, **192,** 503–16 (1964); Specific learning difficulties in childhood. *Pub. Health* **79,** 70–80 (1965).

CHAPTER 8

Find out if the Child likes the Teacher: Personal Dimensions

SO FAR we have treated the problems of reading difficulty as though the child was an object to be studied, described or manipulated. In this chapter we shall take a different view and see how the child seen as a subject, in his own right, must be understood in order to understand his reading difficulties. We shall also adopt the point of view that the ability to read is a *social* skill and that learning to read is part of the totality of growing up and living. Reading and learning are not isolated topics: they are part of life. We need to examine the dynamics of growth and work out how learning to read fits into the overall pattern.

Professor George Kelly,* who developed "Personal Construct Theory", was once asked how his theory could be related to the problem of the child who failed to learn to read. His answer was: "Find out if the child likes the teacher." On the surface this answer is surprisingly naïve, but like most naïve statements it reflects a much deeper truth. In this instance it provides a key to dimensions of understanding which are probably more important than any of those we have so far discussed.

If we accept the view that learning to read is an activity which is part and parcel of living, we have to ask the question, how or why does a child undertake those activities which he does? Even for the child, life does not stand still: he is presented with, or himself creates, situations which call for some action. He may elect to do nothing, he may elect to undertake one of a number of

* KELLY, G. A., *The Psychology of Personal Constructs*, New York: Norton, 1955.

68

choices. We need to be concerned with what it is that determines the choices that he makes and the activities which he masters.

We have in mind at this point the child aged about 5 years who is starting school. He will be presented with a wide variety of activities which he is expected to undertake and the opportunities to acquire a large number of skills. Some of these will involve difficulties which he will be expected to overcome. Some may seem to him to be irrelevant and some will seem to be too simple. All of these activities need to be incorporated into the child's overall development and growth. Learning to read is one of these activities, and he will soon find out that grown-ups consider it to be an *essential* activity. Although the importance which adults attribute to reading will have considerable weight, the child will need to make sense of it for himself as an activity in which he can profitably be engaged.

By the age of 5 years he has already developed skills of communication, both verbal and non-verbal (looking pleased, sulking, crying, etc.), and these skills are shared with others, particularly his parents. He is also aware that he is to some extent separate, and different from his parents and his siblings. He has not, however, completed the separation, nor fully defined his own identity and autonomy (Kahn*). Life, in his school years, provides the experience within which this process can take place (cf. Meier†). For the child, therefore, although he could not verbalize this, the acquisition of an identity of self and the awareness of others are major occupations of living.

How does this take place? Following Kelly's ideas, we can say that the child develops this self-awareness and self-conceptualization by learning to anticipate events. For the child the most important events stem from persons: at the pre-school stage his parents, but progressively, after he commences school, his teachers. His own behaviour also constitutes events which have

* KAHN, J. H., *Human Growth and the Development of Personality*, Oxford: Pergamon, 1965.

† MEIER, H., *Three Theories of Child Development*, New York: Herper & Row, 1965.

implications which have to be anticipated and he learns this from the actions and reactions of other people. For Kelly an act may also be construed as a question, and a child's behaviour may constitute a series of questions, the answers to which provide the child with the basis for determining his own future behaviour. The child acquires and confirms his knowledge of self and others by noting and anticipating the reactions when he does things and when others do things. Life is an extended experiment. The acquisition of language gives the child some predictive skills in the world of objects since words represent reasonably stable sets of categories. "Table" for the child means substantially the same as "table" for parents and "table" for teachers. Knowledge of himself, however, is to a great extent dependent on the behaviour of others, what they say and do, in response to the questions which are asked by his own behaviour. These others, his parents and teachers, and at times his peers, become significant determinants of the choices a child makes in his life.

The acquisition of identity is at the same time intimately related to the activities which the child can or cannot do. In mastering new skills and in persevering in new activities he develops a positive self-identity through the approval of significant others, parents, teachers and peers. If a child masters a skill, which gains the approval of his age mates and the disapproval of adults, he very soon learns a number of implications of his and their behaviour. If he can spit further than any other boy, then he will be careful where he demonstrates that skill. If an activity causes apprehension (e.g. climbing high trees), he will soon recognize the effect of this on his parents and will modify his behaviour according to circumstances. Approval or disapproval is the surest sign that an activity can be persisted in or desisted from. For the child, therefore, the choice of activities will very much depend on the patterns of approval and disapproval of adults. When knowingly he incites disapproval he may be making a statement of hostility, or asking the question, how far he can go, or asking a different question, e.g. "was previous disapproval contingent upon a special set of circumstances?" In this way he learns the limits of his independence and also the bounds of his identity and the way that consequences are related to circumstances. When *unwittingly* he earns his approval he may feel puzzled or guilty because either he has not clarified his own self-image or because the image that he has of himself is not the one that others have of him. In the special case of his activity being ignored he does not know whether or not he can persist and he will have to experiment further in order to find out.

The child's sense of identity, his feeling of worth, and, therefore, the activities with which he will be expected to persist, are very much dependent on those adults who are able to provide recognition, approval or disapproval. Recognition alone may be the sole validator of identity. These adults are, of course, the parents, the extended family and teachers. His identity and activities within his peer group are, in the same way, dependent on his siblings and his mates. At times his recognition by this group may be more important than that of the adults. It certainly becomes more important as the child grows older.

We can now use this model in connection with reading and reading failure. As we indicated in Chapter 6, some families do not share the same *aspirations* as the schools and therefore do not present to the child the models that are maximally consistent with what the schools would like. The *activities* which these families will encourage are less likely to be those that the school would encourage, and the activities which the school would like to foster may be irrelevant to them. Learning to read may be one of these activities. Even if parents give verbal encouragement their manifest lack of concern in terms of their own involvement is likely to be the more powerful validator of the child's own approach to the specific activity of reading. Where this happens it is the teacher who must take on the role of the significant adult who, by his own activities, provides the necessary affirmation for the child to persist and master reading.

In areas where families are less concerned about education and do not understand the role of the teacher, the children are frequently warned to do what the teacher tells them and to keep out of trouble. If they do not they "will be punished by the teacher". In consequence the child is likely to see the teacher primarily as a figure to be feared. This is hardly an appropriate image for the person who is to be the main validator for the child's school activities. Fortunately, this negative image is usually overcome by the establishment of a new relationship which the child makes with the teacher. When this happens, what the teacher values will be seen by the child as good. Frequently, however, when children with reading difficulties have been asked who will be most pleased when they can read well, they did *not* name their class teachers. For these children, therefore, the teacher had not become a positive source of validation in their learning activities.

Different adults who are important to the child often have different expectations of him. Parents, in the light of their own expectations, may have succeeded in developing, and seek further to develop, a role and identity for the child which is different from the role and identity which a teacher aims to foster. When this happens the child may be put into the position of having to meet opposite expectations from adults both of whom are valued. His choices in such a situation can never be satisfactory since to meet one set of expectations is to be disloyal to the persons holding the other expectations. The outcome for the child may be a division in his development, with a corresponding failure in developing satisfactory relationships. Or he may withdraw himself mentally or physically from school, and from learning. He may show disturbing behaviour, often unpredictable, which will reflect his confusion.

When the parents are opposed to school and learning, we have one type of situation. On the other hand, when the parents have built up the boy to believe that he is capable of more than his abilities would allow, we have a different sort of situation. Here the teacher will invalidate the child's image of himself and, in the process, will almost certainly invoke the child's hostility. Why should he do the simple things a teacher wants him to do when, in the eyes of his parents, he can do all these things with ease? In fact, the child will fail to learn and, more importantly, will not see the need to learn. And in any case he will not construe his teacher in favourable terms, with the result that the teacher will lose any positive value for the child and only have negative value as an inappropriately punitive authority figure.

These possibilities are very real at the start of the child's school life. If the contradictions are not resolved in the early stages, the sequel can be very bad. Persistent experience of failure will produce an identity of failure and lead to expectations of continued failure in those activities which the teacher demands the child should master. The failure may be total or in a specific subject, e.g. reading. A parallel exists in adulthood. Many women accept an identity which includes failure in manipulating numbers and calculations and they will usually say that they were no good at mathematics in school. Failure in mathematics in an adult can be lightly admitted, not so failure in reading. The manner in which self-identity includes the capacity to read and to use numbers contributes to the development of self-esteem.

When the identity of failure is well developed, the question must be asked, what the implications are if the child succeeds. Will he, by gaining the approval of the teacher, sacrifice the esteem of his friends who still cannot read? Dare he seek the approval of the teacher if he realizes what this may cost in the eyes of his friends, who are unable to gain that approval? The assumption that success always pays is not necessarily true. It is not infrequent that, when a child succeeds in one area, he may think that he must succeed in other areas. This can be inhibiting, since it may involve the child in changes of identity which are too far-reaching for him to accept with equanimity. As an example, a 7-year-old child who has acquired some reading skill may be expected by his parents to take on further responsibilities for his younger siblings. This, however, may be felt as a diminution of freedom, or a premature taking on of some aspects of adult activities. Whilst many children welcome this development of identity, others might prefer not to. And in order to avoid this particular set of implications of success, they become "reluctant" learners. Such attitudes, which may have their roots in events in early infancy, are very difficult to modify.

A further aspect of this same dimension stems from the fact that a child is aware that he is growing up. He learns this from his parents, his teachers, his siblings and his age mates. Learning to read is part of this process of growing up and most children accept the responsibility eagerly. Sometimes, however, growing up may present for the child a threat that he finds difficult to accept. He anticipates a role for himself as a grown-up, but his perception of the grown-ups is of those he already knows, notably his parents. They may be mentally or physically ill, they may be cruel to one another, they may be creators of misery, they may be people who present adult life as a burden and school life as bliss. In such circumstances, the child's approach to anything related to growing up, including reading, is negative, or is charged with anxiety or perhaps with hostility. The choice for the child is whether or not to undertake activities which are related to growing up, and his experience and anticipations lead him to reject growth.

A case will illustrate this problem. Peter had been seen at the child guidance clinic when he was 5 years old on account of his disturbed behaviour. The family withdrew after a few interviews. At the age of 8 years he was investigated in school as he was not learning to read. Suggestions were made to the teacher which took account of Peter's pattern of cognitive ability but Peter continued not to learn. At the age of 10 years Peter was seen again in school as the head teacher felt that the boy would not be able to cope in the secondary school. By this time a social worker was also involved in the case as the mother was mentally ill. The evidence which was now available showed that the mother was unable to go out of the house, but in fact ruled the family with her illness. The father had doubts as to whether or not he was a homosexual, and presumably had doubts also as to his effectiveness. Peter's main enterprises in school were to please the teacher but not with academic achievement. In fact, when he gave answers which received praise he immediately retracted them and would frequently become enraged. This boy dare not accept as part of his identity attainments and skills which were for most children a normal part of growing up. The models which his parents provided, the mother who could not go out and the father who had doubts about his masculinity (perhaps encouraged, if not sown, by the mother), were hardly such as to encourage Peter to grow up in a normal manner. His failure to learn in fact strongly suggests his rejection of growth, and he will be unlikely to learn unless he leaves home and goes to a residential school.

The same rejection may take place for other reasons. Some parents have actively discouraged the child's exploratory and experimental behaviour. They have taken decisions out of his hands and allowed him neither to anticipate nor to validate the outcomes of his own behaviour. These children cannot know the success and failure of their own ventures. They are prevented, by their parents' interventions, from growing into something more than they are now. But school provides the first area of engagement with life outside of the family and these children are completely unfitted for it. They remain enclosed within a circle created by their acceptance of the attitudes communicated by their parents. Their encounters with teachers are likely to be fruitless. The child is not able to broaden his perception of other adults and therefore cannot develop a working relationship with them. Their encounters with other children are likely to lead to hostility or to complete withdrawal. Just as in one case the parents' interventions have inhibited the child's willingness to explore, so the excessive tie between parent and child in the other case inhibits the development of ties with other people. The child therefore has no means of confirming and broadening his own identity. Yet the child needs to give up some of his sense of identity with the parent in order to gain a valid identity in his own right. Learning to read is a key activity in this process since to read means to have access to knowledge which in fact is validated independently of the parent by the teacher. But the teacher cannot be a validator for the child unless he can experience some relationship with her. And this is the one thing that the parents' hold denies.

There is an equally serious corollary to this. A child with sufficient strength will rebel against the parents' hold, but the ways in which this can be achieved are limited. Where reading is a valued activity in the home, however, the rebellion can show itself in a refusal to learn to read. This is a socially acceptable form of rebellion since no one can prove that the child does not have "difficulty" with reading. The child does not show this behaviour deliberately, but to use the expression "unconscious" is not helpful. He does recognize that failure in certain activities meets with parental concern and this may be sufficient to justify him in continuing with these failures. Reading resistance is easily developed along these lines and it is not surprising that specific remedial help is unlikely to be of any value unless at the same time the child can find other ways of expressing his resentment. So long as reading is tied to, or provides a partial solution to, problems in the child's relationships with significant other people, so long will direct help in reading fail. Reading needs to be divorced from other problems so that the child is free to undertake it as a normal part of growing up. It is easy for adults to assume that reading is an activity which all children will take up readily and willingly just because the assumption is valid for the majority of children. When, however, we are confronted with children who continuously fail, it becomes essential to examine the dimensions we have just described in order to understand the implications of reading success and failure for these children. And these implications will be closely related to the child's perception of the people who are important in his life. Nor should it be assumed that when the child is distressed about his reading failure it is because he cannot read and would like to. It may well be the case that it is the implications of reading vis-à-vis himself and others that is causing the distress.

Thus, Kelly's answer "*Find out if the child likes the teacher*" carries also the further corollaries "*Find out if the teacher, or parent, likes the child, and at the same time is not forcing the child into a role which is inappropriate, and is not depriving the child of the means of developing his own identity in a constructive way, nor using the child to meet his own needs"*. These are fundamental questions which must be asked if we are to understand some of the personal and personality aspects of reading failure.

CHAPTER 9

An Overview and its Inverse

WE HAVE surveyed reading and reading difficulties in a number of different dimensions. It is necessary now to put these dimensions into a perspective in order to give a general picture of them. We could start from any single dimension and proceed to relate the others successively to the first. For example, if we see learning to read as a purely cognitive skill we could start with intelligence. Or we could follow the notion that learning to read is merely learning the relationship between sound and visual symbol (cf. Elkonin*). Were we interested in dealing with reading from an administrative point of view we might start with the dimension which emphasizes the role of the school and the teachers.

Our choice of starting-point stems from two considerations. The first is that we see reading as a social skill which is acquired as part of a developmental process. This process starts at birth and leads, through the acquisition of language and skills of verbal communication, to the learning of reading itself. The second consideration is implicit in the findings of the Plowden Report on the primary school. This report indicated that the major determinant of school achievement (and this achievement was to a great extent reading achievement) was the attitude of the parents. Although it has always been recognized that parental attitudes were important, the researchers were surprised that variations in these accounted for more of the variation in achievement than either parental circumstances or variations between

* ELKONIN, D. B., *The Psychology of Mastering the Elements of Reading in Educational Psychology in the U.S.S.R.*, London: Routledge & Kegan Paul, 1963.

schools. In the light of these two considerations we feel it is appropriate to consider the problem of reading within the context of the child's growth within the family and the extension of his development within the schools. This will provide one basic set of dimensions which will then have to be related to another set in which the child is seen as an "information processing" organism. Neither set of dimensions is complete in itself, but each is related or acts as a complement to the other.

In Chapter 5 we discussed some of the sociological and family factors which were related to reading, but it is necessary to broaden this discussion in order to understand more fully the role of the family for the child's development and learning. The argument is taken from the formulations of Lidz *et al.** which in turn stems from theories of the family derived from sociology. Lidz's argument has proved fruitful for understanding some aspects of schizophrenia and it may well be useful in understanding other forms of maladaptation.

The basic proposition is that the family's roles in shaping the child's development are threefold.

The first role involves the provision of parental care and nurturance. This includes material provision, continuity and care. Against this background the child can pace his own development against the relatively stable figures of the parents. At the same time the family provide not only physical and nutritional resources but the element for relational and cognitive growth. It will be recalled from Chapter 5 that maternal care was a major factor in determining the level of school achievement.

In the second role the family is a social institution which provides the basis for the child's early learning of his role, i.e. his sex identification and the sort of child he is within that sex. The process starts in fact before the child is born since the parents will have developed expectations and notions whilst the child is *in utero*. The parents' responses to the child's developing identity will either confirm or disprove that identity according to their

* LIDZ, T., FLECK, S. and CORNELISON, A. K., *Schizophrenia and the Family*, New York: International University Press, 1965.

own expectations. The institution of the family allows or inhibits explorations in different areas of experience which will establish for the child those activities which are relevant or irrelevant to the family. This in turn will determine what is relevant for him. The identity which the child acquires within the family provides the identity with which he starts his school life. The extent to which this identity is subject to modification will be the extent to which the child will be able to accept the schooling and all that it entails.

In the third role the family provides the first training in skills of communication both verbal and non-verbal. The former is, of course, fundamentally important in learning to read, but the latter is also important since it will partly determine the nature of the understanding which can be developed between the child and his teacher and the child with his age mates. In this context, i.e. of communication skills and techniques, the work of Bernstein which was reported in Chapter 6 is very relevant.

Deficiencies in these three roles are likely to affect the ability of the child to cope adequately with the infant schools and the activities which children are expected to master.

The school itself, however, also has a function in these three areas. The area of nurturance and care is satisfied by the provision of adequate material resources and personal concern for the children. Failures here stem from the school's not providing adequate and appropriate stimulus for the child. This is especially important at the cognitive and sensory level since ability, whether general or special, is likely to be adversely affected if the child is not presented with the right kinds of experience.

As an institution the school provides a stable environment in which the child has further opportunities to develop his identity against the continuity which teachers provide. His social identity also develops from his interaction with his age mates, and here again continuity is maintained by the child's remaining with the same group in his class over a period of time. The patterns of approval and disapproval, recognition and non-recognition, which teachers develop for each child will enable the child to recognize what is valued and what is not valued. That is, he will recognize the activities which will meet with approval or disapproval if he succeeds or fails. These patterns will also help to define for the child his own identity and therefore his self-acceptance.

Finally, the school is entrusted with the task of further developing the child's skills in communication, and this includes learning to read. In fact the school may feel that this is its main task. But reading itself provides one of the major bases for bringing to the child the culture of the country and that necessary knowledge which it is felt the child needs to know so that he may become an educated and social adult, prepared as a citizen, prepared to meet the world.

If the school fails in any of these areas, children are likely to be at a disadvantage in learning. Lack of adequate materials, lack of adequate staff, lack of suitable instructional techniques will affect the extent to which any given child will learn or fail to learn. More importantly, however, we need to recognize the fact that the provision of the schools in these three areas needs to be aligned with the provision and preparation made by the parents. Where school and family are at cross purposes in their ideals and expectations, the child is confronted with the situation in which his loyalties are divided. In consequence he may withdraw from the learning situation, he may "go through the motions" of learning, but learn nothing. He may express his conflict by hostile behaviour. He will certainly have difficulties in learning. Where the materials which the school offers bears little or no relationship to those which the child has been accustomed to, he will not get the maximum benefit from them because he will not know how to use them. Where the communication skills are too far removed from those of the family the child will have difficulties in understanding the transactions between teacher and child. Thus, the formative influence of the family, the formative influence of the school, and the interaction of these influences will be basic determinants of what any child will achieve. When he fails, these influences need to be investigated.

This discussion, however, has drawn attention to only one part of the problem. The child needs also to be considered from a different point of view because the influences we have described do not operate in a vacuum.

The child can at this point be seen as an organism which has the potentiality for developing an "information processing system". This system we usually call intelligence. At birth the child is equipped with a brain and with organs which are sensitive to a wide range of stimuli—sound, sight, touch, movement, smell and sensitivity to the workings of his own body. With this equipment the child gradually learns to make sense out of his environment, and, in fact, to think beyond the concrete to the abstract, and beyond the present to the future. He learns to master skills which enables him to use his environment constructively and to meet his own needs and the needs of others.

The quality of this intellectual apparatus varies. Some children are well favoured, others not so well, and some are extremely ill favoured. The variations are frequently determined genetically, but often also by physical factors operating during pregnancy, or by factors arising at birth and, sometimes, by illness in infancy. The effectiveness of the "information-processing system", however, will to a great extent be determined by the total environment into which the infant child is born. By total environment we mean what the parents provide physically, emotionally and intellectually, what the parents encourage and what they discourage. The development of intelligence in fact is very dependent on the experiences which a child undergoes and this is very much determined by the family and what it offers. When we attempt to measure "intelligence" we are in fact attempting to assess the quality of the "information-processing system". In practice the child acquires skills, techniques and strategy for coping with his environment, together with a store of information which may or may not be relevant in achieving this end. What we measure as intelligence is a sample of these skills and this information.

Gross failure of the system can be recognized in children who are *severely subnormal*, lesser failures can be recognized in children who are called *educationally subnormal*. Children who, on the other hand, are academically very bright have available a wide number of skills and strategies and these usually reflect high-quality "information-processing systems". When we are confronted with reading failure we ask if in fact the child has the general ability to learn. If he has not, we accept slowness in learning as normal. If the child's general information-processing ability is good we recognize the child as retarded and ask the further question, Why? In Chapter 4 we discussed this aspect of reading failure and showed something of the relationship between different aspects of intelligence and reading ability. We also discussed some of the information-processing models which related specifically to reading. In the light of these models we may be able to recognize specific intellectual handicaps which will affect a child's ability to learn. And if we can recognize the handicaps it may be possible to devise programmes which will overcome them. We seldom know, however, if the handicap was present at birth or if it has arisen from differential cognitive development. We do not know if such a handicap is the "cause" of reading difficulty. It may only have provided an area of difficulty for the child which laid the basis for a reading difficulty which arose itself as the outcome of other problems with which the child was confronted. It is likely that the cognitive difficulty will become more marked with increasing recognition of reading failure by the child himself.

In summary, therefore, any given child must be observed along a number of different dimensions. He is primarily an individual who has been moulded by the family milieu in which he has developed. The family itself will be a reflection of the cultural group within which it is a member. The child acquires skills of coping and understanding which jointly reflect the quality of his "information-processing" ability, and the experiental "input" which the family has provided. When the child starts school he is subject to a separate set of influences, perhaps representing a different set of cultural expectations. When family and school influences are congruent it is likely that the child will do well. Where they are in opposition, or are unrelated, the chances are less good. The quality of the child's "information-processing ability" or intelligence will play a major part in determining how far a child will go, so long as home and family expectations are congruent. Selective weakness in "information processing" may lead to reading retardation, but not necessarily. Much will depend on the presence or absence of other problems centred on family or school with which the child has more presented. Poor "information-processing ability" will also lead to reading difficulty. The extent to which both the parents and the school provide adequate nurturance, adequate opportunities for developing a positive self-image, and adequate techniques of communication will also determine what the child will achieve. Those children who are likely to have personal problems are likely to be those who will be most affected by failures of the school in these three roles. There may initially be some failure in information processing, but the underlying issues may well be elsewhere. Reading failure may be a simple matter of relatively poor ability or, on the other hand, it may be necessary to see reading failure within a very wide context involving many dimensions.

Thus far, however, we have presented an overview which examines the relationship of factors and influences operating on the child as though he were an object. We need to attempt to see the issues from the child's own point of view. This represents an inverse of the overview.

The child starting school is faced with problems which are new to him. He has to respond to different objects, a different time scale, a wider spatial extension and new people. The most important of these is people. Novelty of such magnitude may be anxiety-provoking and threatening, less so when the child has been prepared for it by seeing the school and the teachers beforehand. The child brings to the new situation the strategies and skills for coping that he has developed within the family circle and these will be the techniques which will guide him in his explorations of all of this newness.

The child knows nothing of the dimensions which we have just been discussing. He does know how some people react to him and to what he does. He knows ways of eliciting approval and disapproval. He does not know yet how the new people, his teachers, will react. He does not know what their patterns of approval are, nor what things they will approve. He does not know the limits of his abilities and disabilities, but he will know something of the meaning of success and failure from his activities at home. He will have expectations of himself that his parents will have fostered. He will not yet know the expectations of his teachers, and he may be worried that they will expect more than he can achieve. He will have some idea of himself as a comic, a cry-baby, a quiet one, a "like his father boy", a troublesome boy and so forth. He does not know how his teacher and his age mates will see him. In face of these doubts it is his behaviour that provides the means whereby he can learn to anticipate situations, events and people. The validators will be his teachers and his age mates, and the manner of validation will generally be approval or disapproval or sometimes just recognition.

In the process, the child will be creating channels for his own behaviour in the light of the responses of others. He will be developing a system whereby he can construe both himself and the world of school. The twin axes of approval and disapproval, recognition and non-recognition, by others will be the two co-ordinates whereby the child learns to chart his way through school life. In the absence of these axes he will be confused. If different teachers use the axes differently he will be confused. He may find that the pattern at home is radically different from that which is used at school. If this happens the child may be confronted with impossible choices and may find self-consistency difficult. He may learn to be a different child according to the situation in which he finds himself.

Within school the child soon finds that there are certain activities which he has to undertake and that these are activities which must be mastered. Reading is one of these activities. The child does not know all the adult reasons for reading, but he will know if his parents value reading by their own enjoyment of it. If they have read to him in his pre-school days, then he will already be prepared to accept reading as a worth while activity. If he has had pleasure from the teacher reading to the class he may also value reading. Apart from this, if he sees the ability to read as an activity which can further his own interests he will undertake it. It may be the case that, in the last resort, he undertakes reading just because the teacher says so. Whatever the condition, much will depend on the attitude of the child to the teacher. As adults we tend not to do things at the request of people we do not like, unless we are compelled to and then we do this half-heartedly. The same is true for a child. If the child does not like the teacher, he is unlikely to engage himself in the activity of reading. If, at the same time, the reading process is felt to be boring and irrelevant the child is likely to do other things which he finds more interesting. He has a scale of values which he brings to his activities, and these will determine how much he will do. The real testing time comes when the child experiences failure in his endeavours, because then he is likely to give up altogether. Here the attitude of the teacher is vital. It is worth remarking that every time the child reads a word aloud, the child is carrying out an experiment. Is the word right or wrong? It is the teacher who validates the child's experiments. Invalidation represents failure, and total invalidation over a long time total failure.

We have discussed the implications of failure in Chapter 8. Persistent failure leads to an identity of a failure, which leads to predictions of failure by both child and adults. This chain of events is difficult to break, but it can be done by the outstanding teacher if the child can be given a new start. Reading failure in an older child starts with incipient reading failure in a younger child age. Unfortunately the child who is retarded in reading is not usually recognized as such until he is 8 or 9 years old.

We have tried to write in some of the dimensions, as we understand them, that a child will use in approaching new situations. We must recognize, however, the difficulty we have in trying to represent the child's point of view. It may well be both more simple and more complex than we can imagine. More simple because he may see things in simple terms, more complex in that we do not know with what fortuitous events he may have to contend.

One fact does, however, stand out clearly. *People* are crucial for the child's learning, whether they are parents, or teachers, or siblings and age mates. The delicate balance of esteem which the child holds for the significant people in his life will affect the manner in which he will persist in, and master, activities with which he is presented in school. The balance is in the child's mind, not in the mind of the observer. When the child succeeds perhaps we do not need to ask questions. When he fails, then *we* must if we are to be able to help.

In summary, we would suggest that a child will persist in and master those activities which:

1. fall within or at the margins of his ability range;
2. are seen by the child to have meaning and relevance to his ongoing life;
3. will meet with recognition as opposed to non-recognition and approval as opposed to disapproval from significant others in the child's life;
4. do not involve the child in conflicting loyalties as between these significant others.

This is a general statement, but learning to read falls into the category of activities which this formulation embraces. When a child starts a new activity these conditions need to be remembered. When a child fails, these conditions suggest the questions which need to be asked.

In presenting both an overview and its inverse we have in mind the fact that when we are confronted with reading failure we are faced with two different but related problems. The first problem is concerned with the professional approach to understanding, or perhaps diagnosing, the bases for the reading difficulty. What are the dimensions which we can invoke to help us clarify the situation, and what are the dimensions which will enable us to take some form of remedial action? The second problem is concerned with the child whom we wish to help. His dimensions are not ours. His knowledge is different from ours. But unless we can make some approximation to the way in which he will learn and the way in which he construes himself, the task and others, we are unlikely to involve him in the remedial process. The overview helps us with the first of these two problems. The inverse helps us with the second. Both are necessary.

Learning to read represents the intersection of many dimensions: the child and the family, the family and the culture pattern; the child and the school, the school and the family; the child and the teacher, the child and his peers; that which the child has to learn and the resources which he has for learning. But primarily reading represents one aspect of the engagement of the child with the life into which he is moving. His success in this venture will be crucial in defining the possibilities which are open to him in later life and in defining his own identity amongst his peers, his parents and his teachers.

Most children learn to read. Many of these might in fact read better than they do. For those who fail we need extra resources of skill, understanding and sympathy. Perhaps we still do not have enough of any of these things.

CHAPTER 10

What Next?

AN ANALYSIS of a problem should, if it is to be meaningful, have some implications for action. This does not mean the laying down of far-reaching panaceas, but rather the indication of some necessary first steps. It is the first steps which are important, and in this final chapter we shall indicate some of the necessary first steps which need to be taken in order to help children who have difficulties in learning to read.

The very first step involves the *recognition* of the child who has learning difficulties. This may seem a rather naïve starting-point but it is essential. It has been known that such children have gone unrecognized until they are 9, 10 or even 11 years old. The responsibility for recognition must rest with teachers and parents and recognition itself depends on the sympathetic observation of, or interaction between, child and teacher, child and parent, teacher and parent. At the simplest level it is necessary for the teacher to observe the child's attempts at reading, and this presupposes that teachers do make a practice of hearing children read. Whilst this is usually what happens in an infant school it is not necessarily so in junior and secondary schools, where, for example, the passive and withdrawn child may not be easily noticed by the teacher. At the level of action reading difficulties exist—but only when they are recognized.

The second step arises from the fact that it is necessary to know the severity of a child's reading difficulty, and whether or not his difficulties lie within "normal limits". But how do we define "normal limits"? It is still probably the case that reading ability (and disability) must be related to age and intelligence level.

This issue was discussed in Chapter 4 and it will be recalled that it is possible to state the range of reading attainment which is normal for any given level of ability at any age if we use the measured relationship between the tests of reading ability and intelligence. A child, therefore, who is recognized as having problems with reading can be assessed on reading and intelligence tests to find out how much he differs in reading attainment from other children of comparable age and ability. The outcome of such an assessment is, in fact, a first step in diagnosis. Two extreme answers can be derived from the assessment: in the first place, the child's attainment may be fully consistent with his measured level of ability; in the second place, the child's measured level of intelligence would lead us to suppose that he could be expected to be reading at a much higher level. In the first case we have the dull child (possibly educationally subnormal) of whom slow progress would be expected in any case. In the second case we have the retarded child, whose poor reading can be seen to be indicative of the need for special help. The discrepancy between the reading level which we would reasonably expect and the reading level which we actually observe is a measure of the child's disability.

This issue, however, presents a third problem. Surely *all* children with reading difficulties need special help, whatever their level of intelligence? Why should the children with a higher level of intelligence receive special help and not those who are of limited ability?

The problem is usually posed in exactly these terms, and the resolution of the problem can also be found in the same language. All children need to be helped in the way which is the most appropriate to their needs. This includes the very bright child who is working well and the dull child who finds school work difficult. Unfortunately, schools often have neither the staff nor the material resources to help each child according to his needs. In consequence, children often do not achieve the levels of academic attainment of which they are capable. If children are recognized as being generally dull, the whole of the educational programme should be related to that dullness. In that sense the educational programme should be special, and learning to read should be an essential part of the total programme. It is wrong to isolate reading from the total context. Children of whom greater achievement might reasonably be expected have, however, manifestly failed in the *ordinary* classroom situation. The highly skilled teacher might be able to help such a child, but in the existing circumstances in most schools this is unlikely to happen. A strong case can be argued, therefore, for the establishment of what, for want of a better label, can be called *remedial reading centres*. A more progressive view would be to abandon the term "remedial", thereby freeing such centres from purely remedial work and allowing them instead to become positive forces for developing techniques in the practice of teaching with regard to reading. Attendance at such centres, whilst primarily for special help to those with difficulties, could also foster interest in the art of reading and in the enjoyment of books generally. Such centres could provide a focus for a variety of activities based on reading for which the classroom itself has too little scope. This proposition, however, is something of a digression.

Having recognized the child who is retarded in reading, by which is meant that he is not reading as well as might reasonably be expected, it is still necessary to know what to do about him. Placement in a reading centre for some part of his working week will be of little use unless there is recognition of and understanding of the child's difficulties. As has been suggested in the argument of this book, his difficulties need to be seen in the context of his whole life and this includes his environment, his family, his special abilities, his previous encounters with the reading task, and his view of himself.

Bruner* draws a distinction between children who have difficulties in *coping* with learning and those who *defend* themselves from learning. This is a fundamental distinction which has to be made. Children who cannot *cope* need help in mastering skills.

* BRUNER, J. S., *Toward a Theory of Instruction*, Massachusetts: Harvard University, 1966.

There is no animosity to the task itself and such children's self-esteem will not have been seriously damaged. Children who *defend* themselves cannot face the implications of succeeding or failing. They need to learn that it is safe to do either. An example will illustrate the point. An 8-year-old boy was referred for failure to learn. As part of the investigation he was asked to put coloured blocks together in order to match patterns which were presented on a card. It was noticed that he kept on saying to himself (and therefore to the investigator) that "It's wrong", even when what he had assembled was correct. He completed two items in this way and took sixty seconds for finding the solution for each problem. The investigator then commented on the boy's verbalization and hazarded the guess that the boy *had* to say that he was wrong, just in case the solution was actually wrong; perhaps he had found in the past that he gave too many wrong answers and got into trouble for it. The boy solved the next problem (which was more difficult) in twenty seconds and actually said that it was right. This boy's performance, in fact, reflected his way of defending himself against the implications of failure and also illustrated the fact that he obtained no satisfaction from the problem-solving activity. His difficulties were not in *coping*, but in approaching the task in a challenging, constructive way. Until he could adopt such an approach he would continue to make little progress in learning. Another boy, engaged in the same task, was able to improve his performance when it was suggested that he imagined the pattern which was to be copied as being divided up into four squares. He had difficulty in *coping* and he could be helped by methods which were directly related to the task itself.

It is not necessarily difficult to distinguish the children who defend themselves from those who cannot cope. One perceptive teacher made the comment that one of her pupils who failed to learn to read was a "pawn in the power game" between his divorced parents. To make matters worse, his father, whom he preferred, was illiterate whilst his mother held a minor secretarial post. This boy (who incidentally had been labelled "dyslexic" by neurologists at a hospital) was able to approach the problem of reading constructively only if the teacher deliberately refrained from teaching him until the boy himself asked for help. Such children need to attend reading centres where a "non-teaching" approach by the teacher is permissible. Children who cannot *cope* may frequently be helped in the ordinary classroom but teachers may find it difficult to give the time which is necessary for the individual child. Where help in learning the process of reading can be given directly it is probably best given by the class teacher.

Yet another category of the total group of children who cannot learn to read, or whose reading is far less advanced than might be reasonably expected, can best be defined as those for whom reading is *irrelevant*. This category is illustrated by the case of a boy aged 10 of superior cognitive ability whose reading (and arithmetic) attainment were at about the 8-year level. On this evidence he was clearly severely retarded. In fact, psychologists in the hospital in which he had been investigated asked if he could be given remedial or tutorial help as he was clearly of "grammar school potential". When the boy was interviewed in school, however, he showed that he was not in the least concerned about reading, and even regretted the fact that he had been led to believe he was capable of high academic success. His interests were geared to adventures (which were unrealistic) and practical activities (where reading did not count). It is doubtful if this boy could benefit from remedial help until he had learned to re-orientate his attitudes to himself and his future.

It is frequently the case that such children lack an adequate "competence" model in their fathers, i.e. their fathers are, within the family, inadequate and uninterested. (In this case the boy's father was described as a vague, shadowy individual, frequently out of work because of "illness".) These children do not see school attainment as purposeful and meaningful activities in their lives, and they are unlikely to be helped until some significant person, perhaps another child or maybe a teacher, provides a model by which they can extend their own activities and interests. Failure for these children is less likely to lead to the development of inadequate self-esteem since their successes, i.e. their validation, are achieved in other areas of life. It is generally true that help cannot be given unless help is felt to be needed. These children do not seem to recognize such a need and consequently direct help will be seen as an irrelevance. Perhaps it is the case that they will become dissatisfied with themselves only when they recognize in some person, whom they admire, abilities and skills which they themselves do not possess. In this sense, *persons* are more important than *special provisions* either by way of special classes or special techniques.

Although three categories can be separately identified it would be a mistake to assume that children can be neatly fitted into these categories without overlap. Children who cannot *cope* may well build up *defensive* attitudes and finally abandon the task as *irrelevant* and meaningless. Children who are *defending* themselves against reading may have cognitive difficulties in *coping* which provide pegs for the *defensive* manœuvres. The lack of *relevance* for these children may be another form of *defence*. The important point to be made is that these aspects of children with reading failure need to be understood by those who recognize the reading difficulties and by those who try to do something about them.

More generally, these same three themes, *coping*, *defence* and *relevance*, are important for *all* children. *Coping* relates primarily to the cognitive or information-processing aspect of children's learning. *Defensiveness* relates to the child's attitude to life in terms of his experimentation with his family, his peer group, his teachers and himself. *Relevance* relates to the value systems of his culture, his family and his school. In this sense, the seeds of reading attainment—and school attainment generally—are sown at birth. They develop throughout his pre-school years and are brought to fruition in his school career. This might seem to be a defeatist attitude, but in fact that is not so. The child's entrance into school provides the basis for a new start which *can* greatly modify the development of the growing child.

The conditions for positive development in school are very much determined by the sensitivity of the teachers to the role of the child within his family, the role of the family within the sub-culture, and the role of the sub-culture in its relationship to the culture of the school and its teachers. This sensitivity cannot be taken for granted. Frequently it does not exist at all. For this sensitivity to be developed requires that teachers need to be involved with parents to a far greater extent than has usually been the case and possibly the involvement needs to start long before the child starts school. This is, of course, one of the recommendations of the Plowden Report (paragraph 130). There will also need to be an ongoing involvement in which communication must be in some respects between equals. Without this basis of equality it is unlikely that parents will be able to speak freely about their own understanding of the child's development. Parents also have difficulty in coping, they also defend, and they also have different value systems. Teachers are not immune either.

Communication of itself will not solve any problems unless the message in the communication can be used constructively in the development of different ways of acting. To do this requires imagination, courage and skill. Frequently the problems will be such that outside workers will need to be involved (psychologists, doctors and perhaps social workers) and consequently teachers need to be willing to share their problems with these outside workers. The emphasis here is on sharing rather than on handing over to another agency. To share problems invites the possibility of mutual growth amongst those who share. To hand over problems inhibits the possibility of growth.

In the same way that when the child starts school he enters a new experimental arena, so the child with reading difficulties entering a reading centre away from his classroom also enters a new experimental arena. Within the new context, it may be possible for him to develop more positive attitudes to himself and his work, especially if the teacher is able to deduce from the child's own behaviour the nature of the underlying difficulties. When children fail to benefit it is less likely to be the child who is at fault than the teacher who has failed to understand, or given the understanding, that the context within which the child is living at home is so harmful as to justify the child's removal to a residential school.

Progress within a remedial reading centre is not, or should not be, the sole aim. For the work to be effective, progress should be maintained in his own school, when the child leaves the centre and returns, full-time, to his own class. When this does not happen it is worth asking the extent to which the remedial agent has been in communication with the class teacher and the extent to which the class itself has been adjusted to meet the needs of the returning child. Research on the effectiveness of reading centres has invariably produced equivocal answers (Curr and Gourley*), and it has been suggested that no case can be made for such centres. On the other hand, there has been little documentation as to how remedial teachers have seen their task, how they have understood the problems and how they may have engineered the return of the child to the classroom.

The tenor of this chapter is that much is to be demanded of the teacher, more perhaps than has been traditionally demanded. Reading difficulties, seen from the teacher's angle, stem from inadequate preparation in the training college since it is during their training that the nature of the demands could first be made known. These demands will not, however, be fully understood until the teacher is presented in school with real children who match their own difficulties to those of the teacher. If the teacher fails, as sometimes he must, who then can help? Outside agencies cannot take the problem from the teacher. Perhaps only a better or more appropriate teacher can. But the teacher need not stand on his own. Within the school, the combined wisdom of the staff can be brought towards a reappraisal of those children whose learning, whether in reading or in all subjects, falls short of what might be expected. When this is not enough, the services of other professional workers can be brought in.

From the experience derived from the special cases of learning difficulty it might be possible to help *all* children to a better

* CURR, W. and GOURLAY, N., The effect of practice on performance in scholastic tests. *Brit. J. Educ. Psychol.* **30,** 155–67 (1960).

realization of their potentialities. It is probable that few children achieve the levels that are possible. In that sense all are retarded. The understanding derived from children who fail may provide the bases for helping children in general to succeed more effectively.

Selected References

BRUNER, J. S. (1966) *Toward a Theory of Instruction*, Massachusetts: Harvard University.

DIACK, H. (1965) *In Spite of the Alphabet*, London: Chatto & Windus.

DOWNING, J. (1966) *The First International Reading Symposium, Oxford, 1964*. London: Cassell.

H.M.S.O. (1967) *Children and their Primary Schools* (The Plowden Report), London: Central Advisory Council for Education (England).

McLUHAN, M. (1962) *The Gutenberg Galexy*, London: Routledge & Kegan Paul.

MORRIS, J. M. (1966) *Standards and Progress in Reading*, Slough: N.F.E.R.

TANSLEY, A. E. (1967) *Reading and Remedial Reading*, London: Routledge & Kegan Paul.

VERNON, M. D. (1957) *Backwardness in Reading*, Cambridge: Cambridge University Press.

VIGOTSKY, L. S. (1962) *Thought and Language*, Massachusetts: M.I.T.

Index